Supply side economics

Third edition

Nigel M. Healey
Manchester Metropolitan University

and

Mark Cook
Nene College

Series Editor
Bryan Hurl, Harrow School

Heinemann Educational Publishers
Halley Court, Jordan Hill, Oxford OX2 8EJ
a division of Reed Educational & Professional Publishing Ltd

OXFORD FLORENCE PRAGUE MADRID ATHENS
MELBOURNE AUCKLAND KUALA LUMPUR SINGAPORE
TOKYO IBADAN NAIROBI KAMPALA JOHANNESBURG
GABORONE PORTSMOUTH NH (USA) CHICAGO MEXICO CITY SAO PAULO

© Rosalind Levačić, 1988
© Nigel Healey and Rosalind Levačić, 1992
© Nigel Healey and Mark Cook, 1996

First published 1988
Second edition 1992
Third edition 1996

00 99 98 97 96
10 9 8 7 6 5 4 3 2 1

British Library Cataloguing in Publication Data
A catalogue record for this book is available from the British Library

ISBN 0 435 33034 9

Printed and bound in Great Britain by Biddles Ltd, Guildford

Acknowledgements

The publishers would like to thank the following for permission to reproduce copyright material.

Associated Examining Board for the questions on pp.15, 24, 25, 26, 42, 43, 44, 52, 63, 74, 86; © S. & C. Calman for the cartoons by Mel Calman on pp.59, 78; Crown copyright is reproduced with the permission of the Controller of HMSO for the tables on pp.9, 67; © *The Economist*, London, 8.6.96 on p.11, 15.6.96 on p.21, 6.11.93 on p.27, 28.3.92 on p.40, 16.4.94 and 3.9.94 on pp. 53–4, 4.9.93 on p.65, 1.6.91 on p.75, 8.6.96 on p.81, 27.5.95 on p.89; Express Newspapers for the Giles cartoon on p.20; Fiscal Studies, August 1991 for the graph on p.54; Northern Examinations and Assessment Board for the questions on pp.15, 25, 35, 43, 53, 63, 74, 86; © *The Observer* for the article by John Grieve-Smith on pp.43–4; © OECD, 1995, Performance of the British supply side, 1963–95 on p.9; Oxford and Cambridge Schools Examination Board for the questions on pp.25, 43, 52, 63, 74, 86; J. Prynn, Nissan Europe, Leicester University MBA, 1993 on pp.25–6; *The Spectator* for the cartoon by M. Heath on p.58; Approximately 430 words (pp.119–120) from Keynes in the 1990s: A return to economic sanity by Michael Stewart (Penguin Books, 1993) on pp.15–16 © Michael Stewart, 1993. Reproduced by permission of Penguin Books Ltd; © Telegraph Group Ltd, London, 1994 for the article on p.26; © Times Newspapers Limited, 1996 for the article on p.33; University of Cambridge Local Examinations Syndicate for the questions on pp.24, 35, 52, 86; University of London Examinations and Assessment Council for the questions on pp.15, 16, 24, 35, 42, 52, 63, 73, 74, 86, 87; University of Oxford Delegacy of Local Examinations for the questions on pp.15, 24, 42, 52; Welsh Joint Education Committee for the question on p.36.

The publishers have made every effort to trace copyright holders. However, if any material has been incorrectly acknowledged, we would be pleased to correct this at the earliest opportunity.

Contents

Preface

Now that the 'new' Labour party acknowledges the importance of supply side economics, the subject has become part of the essential economic philosophy of both Right and Left politically.

Trying to find a boundary line to this umbrella phrase to determine what to include in a book is like pushing on a piece of string. However, in this third edition there are two major changes over the last. There is a three-chapter core of labour market, taxation and privatization, to which has been added a chapter on important secondary themes. In keeping with the needs of the new syllabuses, the 'difficult' sections have been stripped out.

This series aims to appeal to schools and colleges where both teachers and those taught are eager to get to grips with the real economy of the UK. This third edition of *Supply Side Economics* applies micro and macro theory in an up-to-date way.

Bryan Hurl
Series Editor

Introduction

'What happens to the supply side will, in the long run, be the main determinant of our economic success.' Nigel Lawson

The term 'supply side economics' was first coined in 1976 to describe economic policies that are designed to influence output and employment through their impact on the supply side, as opposed to the demand side, of the economy. *Supply side policies cause a shift to the right of the aggregate supply curve, leading to greater output at lower prices*, so long as the economy is below the full-employment level.

Although the term 'supply side economics' is relatively new, however, the basic concept is not. Ever since 1945, Labour and Conservative governments have attempted to strengthen the supply side in their quests for more rapid economic growth.

Until 1979, however, supply side policy took second place to demand management policy. While successive governments recognized the potential benefits of directly promoting the supply side of the economy, it was generally believed that the major contribution governments could make to economic prosperity was to keep the economy as close as possible to 'full employment' – through the active use of *demand-management policy*. By ensuring that aggregate demand was always high enough to allow firms to work at full capacity, it was argued, governments could create a stable and supportive economic environment in which firms had the confidence and incentive to invest for growth.

In the period 1945–79, supply side policy thus played an essentially supporting role, with governments intervening directly in the supply side in areas where a high and stable level of aggregate demand did not, of itself, appear to be sufficient to stimulate investment and growth.

Underpinning both demand management and supply side policies during the so-called 'Keynesian era' was a deep-seated distrust of the free market and a feeling that the 'invisible hand' was unable to coordinate economic activity and achieve growth. Without the active involvement of paternalistic government, it was argued, it would be impossible to achieve economic success.

Thus demand management policy was considered so important because it was felt that, in the absence of compensating adjustments in

1

monetary and fiscal policy, the level of aggregate demand would tend to fluctuate wildly, rarely reaching the level necessary for full employment.

Similarly, supply side policy took the form of intervening in the decision-making of the private sector, on the grounds that such decisions would otherwise be irrational and shortsighted.

This pessimistic view of free markets was successfully challenged by the *New Classical economists* in the late 1970s, who provided the intellectual inspiration for the economic policies that have been pursued since 1979. The New Classical economists reasserted the power of free markets to deliver economic prosperity, denying that governments could systematically increase output and employment through the use of either demand management or interventionist supply side policies. They argued that demand management policies ultimately resulted in inflation, concluding that such policies were futile and misguided.

More radically still, they rejected Keynesian notions of *market failure,* claiming that the best way to strengthen the supply side was not via direct government intervention but rather by cutting taxes and liberating otherwise vital market forces from cloying state bureaucracy.

Although Keynesians and New Classical economists remain sharply divided over the appropriate role of government in the economy, *both schools of thought agree that the subject matter of 'supply side economics' is the economics of growth.*

Chapter 1 examines Britain's supply side performance, both relative to historical trends and in comparison with our major trading partners.

Chapter 2 explores the determinants of economic growth, highlighting the role of training and education, capital investment and technological progress.

Chapter 3 reviews traditional, Keynesian approaches to supply side policy, which were predicated on the assumption that slow growth was due to market failure.

Chapter 4 outlines the New Classical backlash of the 1980s and 90s, in which privatization, deregulation and liberalization were prescribed as the key elements of supply side revival.

Chapters 5–8 then appraise the performance of recent supply side policy in a number of key areas: labour market reform, tax reform, privatization, and competition and reform of international markets.

Finally, we offer some insights into the likely evolution of supply side policy for the rest of this century.

Chapter One

The UK's supply side performance

'Other countries have far greater problems than we have.'
Sir Edward Heath

Introduction

Politicians and economists often talk about the 'supply side' of the economy. Ministers claim that their policies are designed to 'strengthen the supply side'. Economists refer to improvements or emerging weaknesses in the 'supply side' performance of the economy. Implicit in such statements is the idea that the 'supply side' *relates to the UK's basic economic competitiveness* – that is, the country's ability to produce goods and services that consumers want, at a price they are prepared to pay.

The simplest way to express the same basic notion in more familiar textbook terms is to think of a simple aggregate supply and demand diagram like Figure 1.

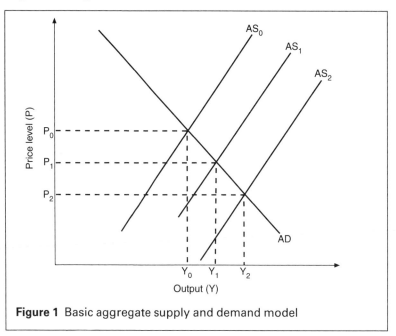

Figure 1 Basic aggregate supply and demand model

- The aggregate supply schedule, AS, shows how much firms in the economy will produce at different price levels, P.
- The aggregate demand schedule, AD, shows the quantities of output, Y, that the nation as a whole – households, businesses and government taken together – want to buy at different price levels.

The 'supply side', therefore, is the part of the economy that lies behind the AS schedule; that is, the companies and workers engaged in the production of goods and services.

From year to year, AD fluctuates up and down, often causing quite sharp changes in total output, Y, which are independent of developments on the supply side. But, in the long run, it is more fundamental changes on the supply side of the economy – such as new products and processes, better educated workers, more efficient plant and equipment – that allow economies to enjoy ever-higher levels of output.

Bitter experience has taught us that, if pumping up demand through higher government spending and rapid credit creation were the route to lasting economic prosperity, the UK would be one of the richest countries in the developed world. But as Table 1 shows, the UK has steadily fallen from its ranking as the richest country in Europe to below average in the European Union.

Table 1 *Per capita* GDP as percentage of EU average

Country	1960	1995
Japan	44.7	186.5
Denmark	123.2	144.4
Germany	123.8	127.6
Luxembourg	158.0	138.8
United States	268.7	123.8
France	126.9	115.5
Belgium	115.4	114.2
Italy	75.2	88.2
Netherlands	97.0	108.7
UK	131.1	87.7

Source: *European Economy*

Within the context of the AS/AD model, underlying improvements in the supply side manifest themselves as a continuous, rightward shift in the AS schedule over time, such as from AS_0 to AS_1 to AS_2, steadily increasing the quantity of output that firms supply at any given level of AD.

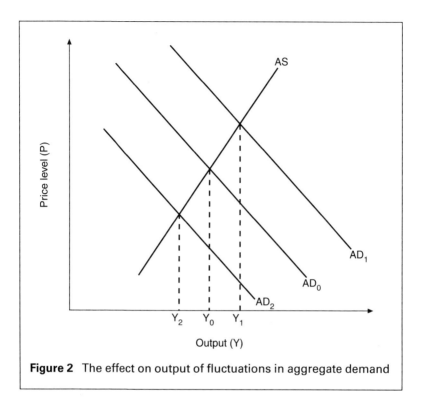

Figure 2 The effect on output of fluctuations in aggregate demand

Somewhat confusingly, when professional economists speak of 'economic growth', they often mean nothing more than the change in output over a short period such as one year. You may have read newspaper reports along the following lines:

> *'The Treasury today forecast 2 per cent growth over the next twelve months'*

> *'The Opposition leader again declared that, owing to the government's mishandling of the economy, Britain will suffer the slowest growth of any major industrial country this year'.*

However, as Figure 2 suggests, changes in economic growth over such short periods are driven primarily by fluctuations in AD – such as from AD_0 to AD_1 or to AD_2.

Output and unemployment

Figure 3 illustrates diagrammatically the cyclical pattern that the economy tends to follow. The broken line represents actual output, while the thick line shows the underlying, long-run growth in the economy's

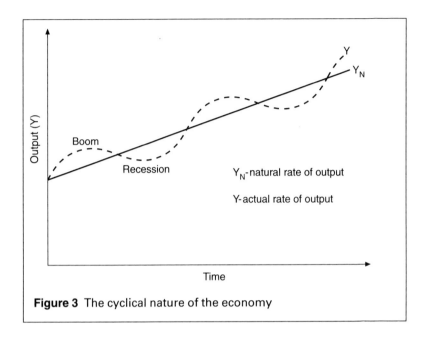

Figure 3 The cyclical nature of the economy

productive capacity. It is this **natural rate of output,** rather than the actual, year-to-year level, which is influenced by changes in the supply side.

During boom years, when the growth of output is accelerating above its natural rate, unemployment steadily falls and actual output is driven above the natural rate of output. Companies have to work nearer to full capacity; bottlenecks appear in the economy; unemployment drops and firms suffer labour shortages, leading them to bid up wage levels; inflation accelerates.

Once the boom has peaked and the economy moves into recession, the growth in output slumps below that of the natural rate, possibly even becoming negative, as in 1980/81 and 1990/91. Unemployment mounts, as many firms lay off unneeded workers; others go out of business altogether; inflation slows.

This account of the **stop–go** (or 'boom–bust') cycles followed by market economies underscores the key relationship on the supply side of the economy between output and unemployment. By now it should be evident that *rising output, of itself, does not signal an improvement in the supply side of the economy.* Any country, provided that it first undergoes a deep recession, can temporarily enjoy a period of 'economic growth', simply by allowing an expansion in AD to mop up under-utilized resources and temporarily propel actual output above its natural rate – whether or not that natural rate of output has in fact increased.

In terms of the supply side of the economy, *what matters is the growth of the natural rate of output; that is, the long-run rate of economic growth that can be sustained over time.* Short-run fluctuations in the growth of actual output, which are mirrored by changes in unemployment – with unemployment falling at times of above-average economic growth and vice versa – tell us very little about changes in the fundamental strength of the supply side.

Labour productivity

A composite guide to the vitality of the supply side is the rate of growth of **labour productivity**. Labour productivity measures the output per worker – that is, total output divided by total employment. We know that output can be increased by reducing unemployment, but unless productivity is also raised, such gains do not indicate any sustainable improvement in the supply side of the economy. *Output per head*, therefore, offers a guide to the performance of the supply side, by effectively 'adjusting' increases in output for any change in the level of unemployment.

Although labour productivity gives a better picture of the trends in the underlying developments in the supply side, its behaviour is, unfortunately, also sensitive to the effects of the economic cycle.

Consider the early stages of a **recession**. Firms may be unsure how long the downturn will last and typically 'hoard' their best workers, choosing to cut output and temporarily pay staff in excess of their marginal revenue product in order to avoid the costs of firing and subsequently rehiring workers when business picks up. As a result, output growth falls, but unemployment initially rises only slightly, so that the early stages of the downturn are characterized by a slowdown in productivity growth.

At the **trough** of the recession, however, firms are forced to reassess their prospects and lay off workers in order to cut costs. In the middle stages of the recession, therefore, while output growth may not slow any further, unemployment will begin to rise rapidly and the productivity of those employees that remain in work rises.

As **recovery** begins to gather pace, firms expand output by using their existing workforces more intensively – for example, by working staff overtime – waiting to be sure that the upturn will be sustained. Output growth accordingly picks up, but with unemployment little affected, productivity growth accelerates further. Only once the recovery is in full swing and firms start taking on additional staff, does

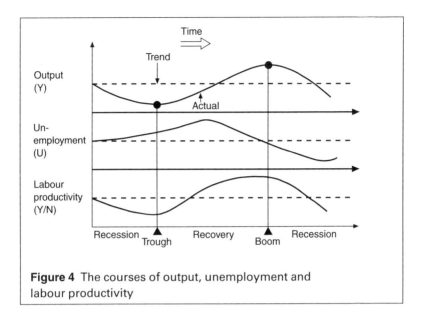

Figure 4 The courses of output, unemployment and labour productivity

unemployment begin to fall. As the economy approaches the **peak** of the boom, productivity growth gradually slows.

Figure 4 illustrates the course of output, unemployment and productivity over the four stages of the economic cycle: recession, trough, recovery and peak.

The UK's supply side performance

Against this background, we can now turn to consider the UK's supply side performance. Table 2 sets out the performance of the British supply side over the last 30 years. It shows that, following a period of unprecedented economic growth between 1963 and 1973 – when output (real GDP) grew more rapidly than at any time since the industrial revolution – the rate of economic growth slowed sharply.

The so-called 'long boom' of the 1960s and early 70s was punctured by the first OPEC oil crisis, when oil prices quadrupled, tipping the world – and the UK – into a deep recession. Since then, while growth has picked up slightly during the period 1979–95, though dipping during the 1990–92 recession, the improvement is slight. It is being constrained during the late 1990s not least by continental Europe as it prepares itself for monetary union.

The picture for the economy as a whole is even worse for the manufacturing sector. Although structural change now means that manufacturing constitutes only about 20 per cent of total GDP (services

Table 2 Performance of the British supply side, 1963–95
(percentage average annual change, year-on-year)

Years (annual average)	Real GDP(%)	Manufacturing output (%)	Labour productivity (%)	Employment (%)	Gross fixed investment (%)
1963–73	3.3	3.6	2.9	0.2	4.8
1973–79	1.5	0.5	1.1	0.2	0.3
1979–95	1.8	0.6	1.8	0.1	2.1

Source: Goldman Sachs; OECD Economic Survey

account for 70 per cent of total output), it continues to generate over half the UK's export revenues and the vitality of the manufacturing sector is crucial to the nation's economic success – as Germany and Japan have graphically illustrated.

Many economists believe that the sluggish growth of manufacturing output, which even by 1995 was not greatly in excess of the 1973 levels, poses grave long-term problems for the British economy. As North Sea oil revenues dwindle, they argue, the UK's consumers will be unable to enjoy the CD players, VCRs and high-tech cars that Japanese and German exporters presently supply, but which domestic companies no longer produce. This theme of **deindustrialization** is dealt with in a companion volume in this series.

Labour productivity growth has also fallen sharply since the long boom. Although the period 1973–79 recorded a dismal annual 1.1 per cent growth in productivity, the improvement since then has been patchy. In the mid-1980s, productivity rattled along at well above 3 per cent a year, encouraging some commentators to conclude that the 1970s had been a temporary departure from long-term trends. But once the recessions of 1980/81 and 1990/91 are taken into account, the underlying trend for the period 1979–95 is not as good as might be expected.

Interestingly, Table 2 shows that employment has grown slowly, but steadily, over the last 30 years. This apparently contradicts the widespread impression that unemployment has been on a relentless upward trend since the mid-1960s. In fact, a combination of demographic and social trends has meant that both rising employment *and* unemployment have occurred simultaneously (see Figure 5).

While the underlying demand for labour has been continuously expanding, at the same time the supply of labour has grown even more rapidly. More and more mothers with young children now work; structural changes in working patterns mean that women who would previously have been forced to stay at home can work part-time;

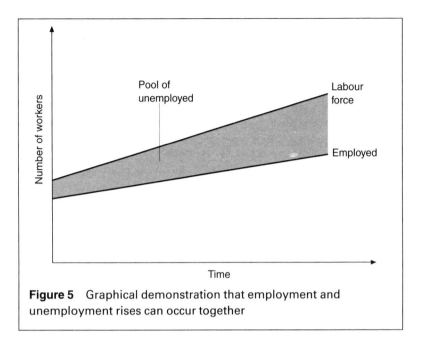

Figure 5 Graphical demonstration that employment and unemployment rises can occur together

'bulges' in the birth rate during the 1960s fed through to cause a temporary 'blip' in the size of the labour force during the 1980s (although this has begun to reverse in recent years).

Finally, the growth in investment has slowed over the last 30 years – although, after virtual stagnation during the period 1973 to 1979, it actually grew rather more rapidly than output (implying that the proportion of GDP invested has risen) between 1979 and 1995. Nevertheless, although the UK enjoyed something of an investment boom during the late 1980s, the increase in the total capital stock since 1979 is disappointingly small. Indeed, in sectors like transport, the capital stock has actually shrunk, rather than increased, over the last 16 years.

International comparisons

In 1970, labour productivity in the UK was equal to that of Germany and almost 50 per cent higher than that of Japan (although only half that of the United States). As Figure 6 shows, over the intervening period German productivity has inexorably accelerated away from British rates, while we have been steadily overhauled by Japan. If present trends continue, *per capita* GDP in the UK will be overtaken by **newly industrializing countries** like South Korea, Taiwan and Singapore before the end of the century.

It hurt, but did it work?

After 17 years of painful Tory reforms, does Britain's economy now hold its own against the best of its international rivals, or is it still falling behind? This will be hotly debated in the general election. Both main political parties are already on the attack. The government is boasting about last week's glowing report from the OECD and a competitiveness league table that put Britain above the big continental European economies.

Labour, meanwhile, took Britain's poor showing in another competitiveness ranking published last week as more proof of economic decline under the Tories. It has been claiming *ad nauseam* that between 1979 and 1994 Britain fell from 13th to 18th in the "world prosperity league table". Who is right?

League tables of economic competitiveness should always be taken with several pinches of salt, not least because economists are split over what, if anything, competitiveness means. Last week's pair of rankings reflects this uncertainty. Each relied on scores of different measures, some quantitative, others qualitative; Britain was ranked differently because the measures used were different. But even the apparently authoritative "prosperity league" quoted by Labour, ranking countries by GDP per head, reveals less than it first appears to do.

According to Labour, since 1979 Britain has been overtaken by Germany, Japan, Italy, Norway, Hong Kong and Singapore, although at the same time it has edged ahead of Sweden. Our chart from the World Bank broadly confirms that. So far, so bad. However, although Labour ranks Hong Kong and Singapore immediately above Britain, they are 5th and 6th respectively in our chart: Britain can take some comfort from not being the only industrial country to fall behind those "tigers".

But arguments about exact rankings probably mislead by suggesting precision. In order to make comparisons, each country's GDP is adjusted to ensure "purchasing power parity" – that is, using the exchange rate which makes the price of goods and services the same in every country. This is more art than science, and a wide margin for error should be applied to any figure, points out Martin Weale, director of the National Institute of Economic and Social Research (NIESR). The differences in GDP per head for those countries between Japan in 7th place and Sweden in 20th are too small for the rankings to be reliable. What is clear, though, is that Britain is no longer falling behind the pack.

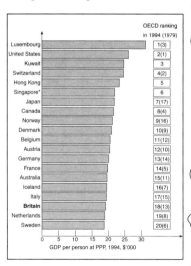

OECD ranking in 1994 (1979)

Luxembourg	1(3)
United States	2(1)
Kuwait	3
Switzerland	4(2)
Hong Kong	5
Singapore*	6
Japan	7(17)
Canada	8(4)
Norway	9(16)
Denmark	10(9)
Belgium	11(12)
Austria	12(10)
Germany	13(14)
France	14(5)
Australia	15(11)
Iceland	16(7)
Italy	17(15)
Britain	18(13)
Netherlands	19(8)
Sweden	20(6)

GDP per person at PPP, 1994, $'000

Abridged from *The Economist*, 8 June 1996

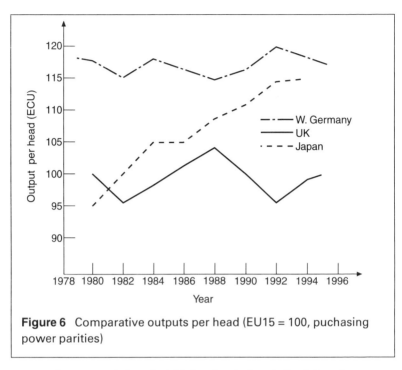

Figure 6 Comparative outputs per head (EU15 = 100, puchasing power parities)

It is often argued that the UK, having industrialized first, has necessarily enjoyed lower growth rates than other countries. While there is some substance in this argument, there is no systematic relationship between *per capita* GDP and economic growth. Once-poor countries like Singapore have enjoyed growth rates that quickly raised their living standards to European levels, and countries like Guyana that were equally poor in 1960 have marked time. Similarly, rich countries like Venezuela – which boasted living standards equal to those in Germany and the UK in 1960 – have stagnated, sliding back into relative poverty. In general, there appears to be almost no relation between *per capita* income and rates of economic growth.

Table 3 compares the UK's supply side performance since the end of the long boom with our main partners in the European Union. It shows that on every indicator, the UK ranks last amongst the 'big four':

- GDP and labour productivity growth rates have been slower;
- relative **unit labour costs** have increased more rapidly (see the box);
- employment growth has been more sluggish;
- gross domestic fixed capital formation has grown more slowly.

Although some of the differences appear small, it is important to

Table 3 Relative performance of the British supply side, 1974–95 (percentage average annual changes year-on-year)

	Real GDP (%)	Labour productivity (%)	Relative unit labour costs* (%)	Employment (%)	Gross fixed investment (%)
UK	1.9	1.8	1.0	0.08	1.5
Germany	2.0	1.8	–0.2	0.3	1.5
France	2.2	2.0	–0.01	0.2	1.2
Italy	2.6	2.0	–0.2	0.6	1.0

*Relative to other EU member states (see box)
Source: *European Economy*

bear in mind the effect of compounding. For example, over the 21 years between 1974 and 1995, the extra 0.3 per cent GDP growth enjoyed by France means that, had the UK and France had the same GDP in 1973, French GDP would now be over 6 per cent higher (in fact, French GDP was already well above British GDP in 1973, so the gap now is even greater).

UNIT LABOUR COSTS

Unit labour costs are equal to:

$$\frac{\text{wage + non-wage costs per worker}}{\text{average product per worker}}$$

Unit labour costs therefore rise when wage or non-wage (e.g. employers' National Insurance contributions) increase and fall as productivity rises.

Relative unit labour costs (RULCs) are unit labour costs expressed in a common currency and related to the average of a group of countries (in Table 3, the EU as a whole). A rise in RULCs implies deteriorating competitiveness, which could stem from:

- a relative increase in wage or non-wage costs, in domestic currency terms;
- a relative decline in the growth of labour productivity; or
- an appreciation in the exchange rate.

Conversely, a fall in RULCs implies increasing competitiveness.

Conclusions

Supply side performance is often taken to be synonymous with economic growth – that is, the rate of change of output. In fact, the rate of growth of output is highly cyclical, typically accelerating during an economic upswing and slowing during recession. It can therefore be misleading to try to infer what is happening to the underlying rate of economic growth from the rate of change of output over a relatively short period. Measuring output growth from the peak-to-peak (i.e. from the peak of one cycle to the peak of the next) gives a better impression of trends on the supply side, but since no two economic cycles are precisely the same, even this approach has important limitations.

Bearing these caveats in mind, over the long run, the UK's supply side performance does appear to suggest that other countries do not have far greater problems than we have. While output has grown at an average rate of approximately 2 per cent a year over the last 30 years, approximately doubling real living standards over this period, in comparison with other developed countries the UK has fared badly. Second only to the United States in terms of *per capita* income in 1960, the UK has steadily slipped down the international league table, as Japan and almost all of the northern European states have overtaken us.

It is to a better understanding of the reasons for the UK's supply side record that the next chapter turns.

KEY WORDS

Natural rate of output	Peak
Stop–go	Unemployment
Labour productivity	Deindustrialization
Recession	Newly industrializing
Trough	countries
Recovery	Unit labour costs

Reading list

Anderton, A., Units 69 and 92 in *Economics*, 2nd edn, Causeway Press, 1995.

Bazen, S. and Thirlwall, T., *Deindustrialization*, 3nd edn, Heinemann Educational, 1997.

Maunder, P. *et al.*, Chapters 14 and 26 in *Economics Explained*, 3rd edn, Collins Educational, 1995.

Essay topics

1. (a) Explain how supply side policies might be used to: (i) reduce the level of unemployment; (ii) increase the rate of economic growth. [70 marks]
   (b) To what extent have supply side policies been effective in achieving these aims in the UK? [30 marks]
   [University of London Examinations and Assessment Council 1996]
2. (a) Why does the level of economic activity fluctuate? [13 marks]
   (b) Discuss the policies a government might adopt to minimize these fluctuations. [12 marks]
   [Associated Examining Board 1993]
3. (a) Examine the role of private sector investment in the promotion of economic growth. [10 marks]
   (b) How might a government seek to stimulate such investment? [15 marks]
   [University of Oxford Delegacy of Local Examinations 1995]
4. Outline briefly the determinants of the level of economic activity in an economy such as the UK. Is it possible for the government to do anything to avoid economic fluctuations or to reduce their effects? [25 marks]
   [Northern Examinations and Assessment Board 1993]

Data Response Question

This task is based on a question set by the University of London Examinations and Assessment Council in 1996. Read the article, which is adapted from *Keynes in the 1990s: A Return to Economic Sanity* by Michael Stewart (Penguin, 1993), and then answer the questions.

> Unfortunately, the economy is not self-stabilising, and if the government assumes it is then there is likely to be trouble. There will be recessions (as in the early 1980s), inflationary booms (as in the late 1980s) and more recessions (as in the early 1990s). The fact is that the economy needs to be managed. If it has been allowed to plunge into recession then, as Keynes argued in the General Theory, the government must step in and increase effective demand.
>
> Reductions in interest rates are a weak and unreliable way of doing this: at a time of recession, the fact that businesses can borrow more cheaply in order to invest does not necessarily mean that they will want to do so. A better approach is an expansionary fiscal policy. What is called for are increases in government expenditure, or cuts in taxation, which will act quickly to increase demand, but which can be phased out or reversed as

the economy comes back to full employment. This expansionary fiscal policy will lead, in the short run, to a bigger budget deficit than would automatically occur in a recession, but there is nothing wrong with that. The extra cost of servicing the National Debt that this deficit will lead to will be small in relation to the rise in output and income that it stimulates. There is no reason why the ratio of National Debt to GDP should necessarily rise.

If there is an unjustifiable structural deficit in the government's accounts – meaning that there is still a deficit when the economy is once again operating at full employment – this will have to be tackled. In the Britain of the 1990s where, it can be argued, public expenditure has been squeezed to such an extent that it threatens many of the decencies of life in a civilised society, taxes will have to be increased. But that is for the future. Tax increases make no sense at a time of recession. What is needed now is a fiscal policy which increases demand, not one which reduces it. Such a policy must be pursued as vigorously as circumstances permit.

Unfortunately, Britain's present circumstances are much less favourable than could be wished. The free market monetarist policies pursued by Mrs Thatcher's government after 1979, based on a dogmatic and exaggerated faith in the virtues of liberalisation, privatisation and deregulation, have led to the emergence of three serious structural imbalances. These restrict the government's ability to bring the economy back to full employment simply by the use of an expansionary fiscal policy. One of these structural imbalances lies in the 'skills deficit' – the lack of skilled labour in relation to the demand for it. A second lies in the chronic balance of payments deficit on current account. The third lies in the high ratio of consumption to output as compared with the low ratio of investment to output.

1. How does the author justify his claim that 'the economy is not self-stabilising'? [2 marks]
2. Explain why the author believes that expansionary fiscal policy would be a better way of increasing effective demand than cutting interest rates. [4 marks]
3. Explain briefly why the author believes that 'Tax increases make no sense at a time of recession'. [3 marks]
4. (a) Why may the 'three serious structural imbalances' restrict the government's ability to bring the economy back to full employment simply by the use of expansionary fiscal policy? [8 marks]
   (b) Examine one policy that could be employed to deal with any one of these structural imbalances. [3 marks]

Chapter Two

The determinants of economic growth

'Economists are interested in growth. The trouble is that, even by their standards, they are terribly ignorant about it. The depths of their ignorance has long been their best kept secret.' The Economist

Introduction
We have already seen that the economy typically moves in a cyclical fashion, with output and unemployment fluctuating over time. These fluctuations can be broadly explained by reference to the behaviour of AD in the AS–AD model in Figure 7.

The economic cycle and changes in aggregate demand
Suppose that AD begins to increase from AD_0. In the short run, money illusion persists and the economy slides up $SRAS(P_0)$. Firms find out-

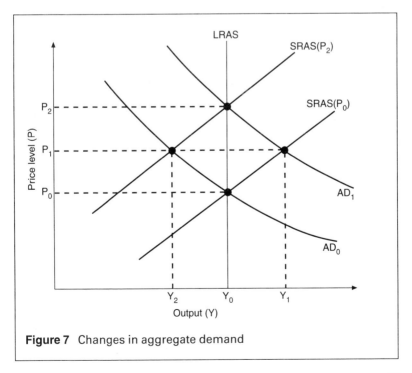

Figure 7 Changes in aggregate demand

put and profits rising, encouraging them to invest in additional capacity; households enjoy rising incomes, inducing them to borrow more and increase current consumption in the expectation of even higher incomes tomorrow. As corporate and consumer confidence rises, the increase in AD becomes self-fuelling, eventually pushing it out to AD_1. At this point, the economy has experienced a sharp increase in real output, from Y_0 to Y_1, at the cost of only a modest increase in prices (that is, inflation) from P_0 to P_1.

Gradually, however, bottlenecks emerge on the supply side. Skill shortages develop in the labour market. And, with the demand for labour strong, as workers begin to realize that inflation is undermining the real value of their wages, unions start to bid aggressively for higher wages. As money illusion fades, the SRAS schedule drifts to the left. A destructive **wage–price spiral** is set in motion as the boom peaks, with the leftwards shift in the SRAS schedule from $SRAS(P_0)$ towards $SRAS(P_2)$ causing output to fall and prices to rise higher still. As profits and output fall, firms cut back investment plans; consumer confidence collapses; and AD shifts leftwards, from AD_1 towards AD_0. Instead of reaching a new long-run equilibrium at P_2/Y_0, the economy instead moves into recession, with output falling below the natural rate, Y_0, to Y_2, until prices and wages adjust sufficiently for confidence and spending to increase once more and set the cycle off again.

It is clear from this account that the original increase in output from Y_0 to Y_1 is not economic growth; nor is the subsequent fall in output from Y_1 to Y_2 a contraction in the economy's supply side potential. Both are simply the results of the fluctuations in AD that appear to characterize free market economies. In contrast, *economic growth implies a sustained increase in the economy's capacity to produce real goods and services in the long run, independent of changes in AD (and unemployment); that is, a rightward shift in the LRAS schedule.*

Economic growth and the long-run aggregate supply schedule

Economic growth thus means a rightward shift in the LRAS – for example, from $LRAS_0$ to $LRAS_1$ in Figure 8(a). At $LRAS_1$, the economy can enjoy more goods and services at any given price level. How could such an increase in the underlying or long-run level of real output come about?

First, consider the labour market in Figure 8(b). If the labour supply were to increase – either because there was an increase in the number of workers available for employment or because the existing workforce offered more hours' labour at any given money wage – this

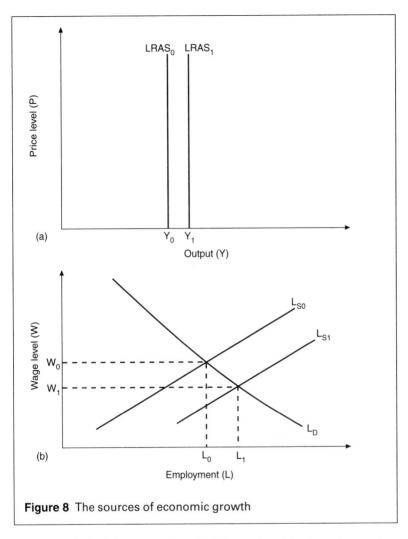

Figure 8 The sources of economic growth

would shift the labour supply schedule to the right from L_{S0} to L_{S1}, raising equilibrium employment from L_0 to L_1. This could be aided if:

- the productivity of labour were to rise, because the 'quality' of labour was increased through better training and education;
- the capital stock were to rise, allowing each employee to produce more output for a given number of hours worked; or
- technological advances were to improve the 'quality' of the capital stock, enabling each worker to produce more output from a given amount of machinery.

During the last century, real output has grown at an average, year-on-year rate of 2–3 per cent. Over this time, the average number of hours worked each week has fallen steadily, while more and more young people have stayed on in school and older workers have retired earlier. Although there have been trends in the opposite direction – most notably an increase in the population and a rise in the proportion of married women working – the growth in the labour force has accounted for only a tiny proportion of the overall increase in output over the last hundred years.

The primary source of the increase in our living standards has been better training and education, capital investment and R & D, rather than ever-harder work. It is to a consideration of Britain's record in each of these three areas that we now turn.

Training and education

The British system of training and education has long been regarded as a root cause of the economy's poor productivity record. Table 4 illustrates that on almost all measures of human capital acquisition, the UK compares unfavourably with the other major economies in

"I have heard that you do not believe there is a shortage of teachers, and that in your opinion there is, in fact, one too many in this class."

Table 4 Percentage of the workforce with vocational qualifications

	UK	France	Germany
University degrees	11	7	11
Intermediate vocational qualifications	25	40	63
of which:			
technician	7	7	7
craft	18	33	56
No vocational qualifications	64	53	26

Source: Trade and Industry Committee (1994)

Europe, and in comparison with both the US and Japan the picture is even worse. Britain has a relatively low proportion of 16–24 year olds in further education and the least educated managerial class in Europe.

The government's recent **skills audit** admits that we come bottom of the class: see the extract 'The unskilled nation'.

The unskilled nation

Sir Humphrey Appleby, the slippery civil servant in the BBC's political comedy series "Yes Minister", would have called it "courageous" – ie, foolhardy. After 17 years in office, and a matter of months before an election, the government has published a detailed study admitting that education and skill levels in Britain are below those in Germany, France, America and Singapore. Unsurprisingly, Labour said it was a damning indictment of the government's record. Gillian Shephard, the education and employment secretary, hopes that voters will give the government credit for its honesty and will recall that, until recently, Labour opposed many of the government's school reforms. She has also announced a package of further reforms in response to the study's findings.

The study, published on June 13th as part of the annual white paper on competitiveness, compared the qualifications held by the British population with those in the four other countries, chosen as key "economic competitors". This "skills audit" found that only 45% of British adults have qualifications that are at least the equivalent of GCSE grade "C" in maths, English and one other subject, worse than in all the other countries. The figure for Germany is 70%. Multinational firms were asked to compare their workers in each country. Confirming the findings of other recent studies, they reported that the British came bottom of the class at sums.

Abridged from *The Economist,* 15 June 1996

Capital investment

Figure 9 illustrates that, expressed as a percentage of GNP, capital investment in the UK falls well below the levels enjoyed in Germany and Japan. The continuing failure of British firms to invest as heavily as their overseas rivals, despite the removal of allegedly restrictive taxes and government regulations, suggests that there may be inherent deficiencies in the way that the private sector functions.

For example, critics of recent policy point to the structure of the British capital market, which – in contrast to those in Germany and Japan – allows companies that do not maximize short-term profits to be taken over against their will. As a result, British management may be deterred from undertaking the investment essential for longer-term economic success, since payback periods are typically long so that investment reduces profits in the short term. Fiscal incentives – for example, tax allowances or capital grants – may be necessary, it is argued, to induce firms to spend on R&D and invest in physical capital in such circumstances.

Research and development

Table 5 illustrates the UK's recent record on R&D. It shows that the proportion of GNP devoted to total R&D was somewhat lower in Britain than in the United States, Germany and Japan in 1991. Moreover, although this is not illustrated in Table 5, it is also the case

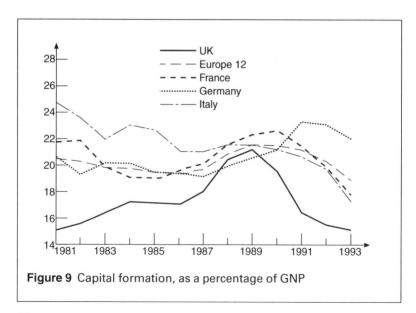

Figure 9 Capital formation, as a percentage of GNP

Table 5 R&D expenditure as a percentage of GNP (1991)

	Total R&D	Of which: Government-funded R&D	
		Military	Civil
UK	2.13	0.14	0.19
Germany	2.65	0.03	0.36
France	2.42	0.18	0.37
Japan	2.93	0.0	0.20
United States	2.78	0.4	0.30

Source: OECD, Eurostat

that while all the other major trading nations increased their share of GNP devoted to R&D in the 1980s, in the UK the ratio actually declined.

An international comparison of gross spending on R&D and output in terms of registered international patents (licences granted to the inventors of new products or processes to protect them from imitation) shows that the UK spent the least of the 'big four' in the EU on R&D expenditure in 1993 (with the exception of Italy) and registered the fewest patents of the five advanced industrial economies.

Conclusions

In this chapter, we have seen that economic growth is a supply side phenomenon. In terms of the AS–AD model, it refers to a rightward shift in the LRAS schedule; that is, an increase in the natural rate of output. The extract reproduced from *The Economist* as the heading to this chapter might appear harsh. After all, we have seen that the basic determinants of economic growth are *not* in dispute. Increases in the labour supply, training and education, investment in physical capital and R&D are unambiguously the prerequisites of supply side success.

But where economists have failed to provide a clear lead is in identifying the factors that influence each of these driving forces that underpin economic growth.

- How does the tax and social security system affect the labour supply?
- Is the best way of stimulating private sector investment in human and physical capital an unregulated, *laissez-faire* environment?
- Is activist demand management necessary to guarantee firms a healthy, growing market for their output and thereby encourage investment and risk-taking?

- What is the role for fiscal incentives – tax allowances and public subsidies – to promote investment and R&D?

Economists have produced no clear-cut answers to these critical questions. Chapters 3 and 4 now explore the basic theoretical differences between the Keynesians, who argue that government intervention is necessary for a strong supply side, and the New Classical school which argues for a deregulated, liberalized economy in which the free market can operate unhindered.

KEY WORDS	
Wage-price spiral	Recession
Economic growth	Skills audit

Reading list

'Economic growth: explaining the mystery', *The Economist*, 4 January 1992, 17–20.

Cook, M., 'Economic growth and the UK economy', *EBEA Journal,* summer 1996.

Essay topics

1. (a) Examine the main factors influencing the level of private sector investment. [50 marks]
   (b) Analyse the significance of investment for long-term economic growth. [50 marks]
   [University of London Examinations and Assessment Council 1995]
2. (a) Explain the benefits a firm might expect to derive from expenditure on research and development. [12 marks]
   (b) Discuss the view that the government ought to provide financial incentives to firms to encourage them to increase their spending on research and development. [13 marks]
   [Associated Examining Board 1995]
3. In 1994 the UK Chancellor of the Exchequer stated that sustained economic growth is only possible if control of inflation remains as the first objective of government economic policy. How far do you agree with this statement? [25 marks]
   [University of Cambridge Local Examinations Syndicate 1996]
4. 'Controlling inflation is easy. Controlling inflation whilst maintaining a high level of employment is impossible.' Discuss, in the light

of recent UK experience. [25 marks]
[University of Oxford Delegacy of Local Examinations 1995]

5. Distinguish between the economic growth and the economic recovery of an economy. Outline the factors to which economic growth may be attributed, and suggest why Britain's growth record compares unfavourably with that of some of the East Asian economies. [25 marks]
[Northern Examinations and Assessment Board 1995]

6. 'The balanced nature of output growth and low inflation suggests that the UK economy has been made more flexible, competitive and less inflation-prone' – OECD, August 1995.
Discuss this statement. [25 marks]
[Oxford & Cambridge Schools Examination Board 1996]

Data Response Question

This task is based on a question set by the Associated Examining Board in 1995. Study the two extracts below, and Table A, and then answer the questions.

Rover in a healthy condition

British car production has increased. This has helped Rover to become the only European manufacturer with increased sales, gaining from the upturn in the UK market where most of its sales are.

The strengths that Rover achieved from its reorganization in the late 1980s have given it the potential to survive and make use of new opportunities. High quality models, including successful executive ranges and the excellent Land Rover division, emphasized targeting of the upper-quality part of different market segments. However, they are threatened by increased imports from Europe, and by the falling opportunities for export to continental Europe. Increased competition from Japanese producers further places their UK share in doubt.

On a global scale, European producers are hampered by lack of overseas markets. Only Volkswagen (VW) has made any impression on American and Japanese markets. Exchange rate fluctuations have not helped either. Internationally, car producers face high overheads which make it difficult to cope with demand fluctuations. Competition is increasing, with global producers expanding into each others' markets faster than the markets can cope with. Europe looks set to be the battleground, as the focus of Japanese expansion shifts from North America, with their production capacity expected to exceed 1.2 million cars a year and sales to rise between 16 per cent and 20 per cent by the end of the decade. Their drive into Europe is hastened by dwindling sales in Japan and a declining American market share and behind the European onslaught lies a battle to survive. The soaring Yen makes their European operations now more efficient. Toyota recently began importing components from its UK factory in Wales (to Japan). Honda plans to sell the Rover Discovery in Japan.

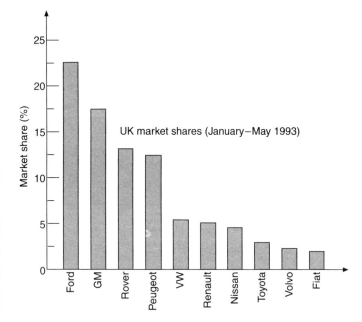

UK market shares (January–May 1993)

Source: Adapted from J.C.R. Prynn, *Can Rover Sustain Their Turnaround in the Changing European Car Market?* (Leicester University MBA, 1993)

Germans buy last major British car maker

BMW is to buy Rover. The new company will be the seventh largest in Europe and about tenth in the world. Although many of the cars produced by the two firms are in competition with each other, they appeal to slightly different tastes. The major attractions for 'cash rich' BMW are likely to have been the Land Rover range, the lower British production costs and the opportunity to develop the Rover models.

Source: Adapted from *Daily Telegraph,* 1 February 1994

Table A Europe's skidding car makers – car sales,
January–September 1993

	Units (000s)	% change on a year earlier
VW Group	1327.2	−22.0
General Motors	1052.2	−11.4
Peugeot-Citroën	1022.5	−16.2
Ford	985.6	−15.3
Fiat Group	962.0	−21.6
Renault	896.9	−15.5
Nissan	285.6	−4.7
Rover	277.5	+12.5
BMW	272.3	−16.4
Mercedes-Benz	243.9	−19.9
Toyota	200.6	−0.4
Mazda	125.5	−24.5
Honda	113.3	−8.1
Volvo	98.1	−16.4
All brands	**8244.9**	**−15.7**

Source: Adapted from *The Economist,* 6 November 1993

1. Compare the relative positions of Rover and Volkswagen (VW). [4 marks]
2. Explain the opportunities Rover might gain from 'the upturn in the UK market' mentioned in the first paragraph of the first extract. [5 marks]
3. Discuss how the exchange rate fluctuations may affect car manufacturers. [8 marks]
4. Using the information provided and your knowledge of economics, discuss why BMW decided to take over Rover in 1994. [8 marks]

Chapter Three

The Keynesian approach to the supply side

'The restructuring of the UK economy must not and cannot be left to the operation of unfettered market forces. What is needed is economic planning. Planning for the market and planning of the market ... which will ensure that all aspects of recovery are properly coordinated – including training, the availability of investment finance and the deployment of technology' Roy Hattersley, formerly deputy leader of the Labour party

Introduction

Until the end of the 1970s, macroeconomic policy in the UK reflected an essentially **'Keynesian view'** of the way the economy operated. Keynesian economists believed, in terms of the aggregate supply and demand (AS–AD) model discussed in the last two chapters, that:

- the private sector components of aggregate demand were very unstable, so that total spending would tend to fluctuate unpredictably in the absence of government intervention; and
- the responsiveness of wages to changes in the price level – particularly in a downwards direction – was very slow.

In particular, Keynesians were concerned that, left to its own devices, aggregate demand might fall, causing the economy to operate below its natural rate of output for extended periods. With wages being **'sticky' downwards**, the economy would therefore suffer persistent unemployment. *This is because wages would not fall to clear the labour market* – which would allow firms to pass on the reduction in labour costs in the form of lower prices, so pushing the economy back towards its natural rate of output.

Keynesians also recognized that spontaneous increases in aggregate demand might equally well lead to inflation, as output increased above its natural rate. However, they tended to regard the possibility of unemployment as the greater danger.

Keynesians recommended that governments should aim to stabilize the level of aggregate demand at the natural rate of output, neutralizing fluctuations in the private sector components of spending by appropriate adjustments in government spending, tax rates and interest rates.

Discretionary fiscal and monetary policy of this type is normally referred to as **fine-tuning**. Not only was this approach to demand management policy urged as the only way of avoiding the twin ills of unemployment and inflation, but Keynesians also argued that stabilizing aggregate demand was the best way to promote economic growth. Because investment in research and development (R&D) and physical and human capital is so sensitive to *expectations* about the future level of demand for firms' finished products, Keynesians claimed that only by ensuring a high, stable level of aggregate demand would firms be able to enjoy the confidence they needed to invest for the future.

Consistent with this view of the world – which was based on the proposition that the unbridled operation of free markets would fail to propel the economy efficiently towards its natural rate of output and unemployment following changes in aggregate demand – Keynesians argued that government intervention in the supply side was also essential if countries were to maximize their growth potential. *In other words, they believed that market failure was so widespread that it could only be tackled via extensive government involvement in the workings of the private sector.*

Market failure and externalities

The intellectual case for market intervention is rooted in basic microeconomics and the concept of **market failure**. The market will fail to allocate resources efficiently whenever the private costs and benefits faced by producers and consumers do not completely reflect the social costs and benefits to society as a whole.

- For example, coal-fired power stations impose a cost on society – in the form of the environmental damage caused by acid rain – which is over and above the producer's opportunity costs such as the cost of land, labour and capital. The additional social cost is known as an **externality** or spillover effect and, being a cost, is negative.
- Conversely, society enjoys a wider benefit from the successful treatment of a patient with a contagious disease – insofar as the risk of other individuals being infected is reduced – over and above the private benefits which accrue to the patient concerned. The extra social benefit is a positive externality or spillover effect.

In both these examples, the presence of externalities will lead to market failure, because the free market will tend to allocate resources in a way that is *socially sub-optimal.*

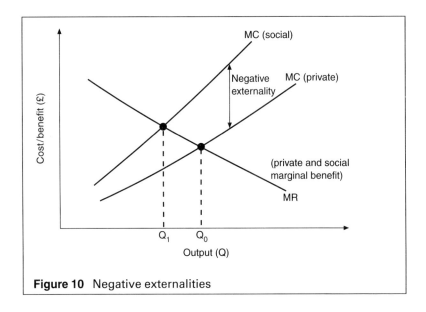

Figure 10 Negative externalities

- Coal-fired power stations will be operated where marginal private cost equals marginal revenue, producing a profit-maximizing amount Q_0 as in Figure 10. In fact, the **social optimum** is where marginal social cost intersects marginal revenue, which would give rise to a lower quantity, Q_1, being produced. In other words, negative externalities result in socially excessive levels of production and consumption.

- On the other hand, the consumption of healthcare by those afflicted with contagious diseases will tend to be less than is socially desirable. Figure 11 shows that utility-maximizing individuals would demand an amount Q_0, which is where marginal private revenue (i.e. marginal private benefits) equals marginal cost. In fact, the socially-efficient level of consumption would be Q_1, where the marginal social revenue (or benefit) schedule intersects marginal cost. Positive externalities thus lead to under-production and consumption.

How do considerations of externalities relate to the supply side? Keynesians argue that many of the key determinants of economic growth are plagued by positive externalities, so that the free market will tend to under-invest in R&D and physical and human capital. As a result, the growth rate will be slower than is socially optimal.

Consider basic R&D. Expenditure on pioneering R&D to develop new products and processes is expensive. Innovating firms are only

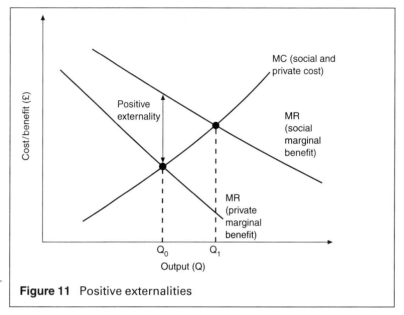

Figure 11 Positive externalities

imperfectly protected by patent laws that are supposed to prohibit rivals from 'cloning' their new products. Patent law is often difficult to enforce and followers have a significant cost advantage over the innovator, since they do not have to recoup the initial R&D costs.

For example, when Sony first launched the 'Walkman' cassette-player it temporarily enjoyed a monopoly position and prices in real terms were 400–500 per cent higher than they are today. Within months of the product reaching the market it was followed by a host of cheaper cassette-players from rival manufacturers, which quickly drove down the market price. Sony's R&D thus had a positive spillover effect from the point of view of other firms. Since Sony could not prevent the technology it had invented from becoming public knowledge, the other firms profited from Sony's R&D without having to pay for it; in other words, the benefit to society as a whole far exceeded the private benefits to Sony.

Given the presence of positive externalities, Keynesians argued, the amount of R&D undertaken by firms in aggregate is likely to be *socially sub-optimal*, with many firms preferring to wait for their rivals to make the technological breakthroughs. It is significant that, in Japan, where the corporate system of *keiretzu* ties together otherwise independent companies through a complex series of interlocking directorships and shareholdings, companies do not have the same incentive to free-ride on the R&D of others – and Japan is a clearly established world leader in high-tech industries. In the UK, on the other hand, Keynesians concluded that the same effect could only be achieved through government intervention.

Training and education may also be subject to similar effects. Imagine that in the absence of publicly provided training and education, a private company decides to offer training services to subscribing firms. While each firm would be paying to send its staff on the training courses, each guesses (rightly) that, by not paying, the benefits can be enjoyed by free-riding at their neighbours' expense, since they may be able to poach trained workers from their rivals by paying only slightly above the present market wage. As a result, many firms refuse to subscribe and the ensuing service is socially sub-optimal.

An alternative solution would be to provide the training publicly, financing it with a tax that each company will willingly pay, in the knowledge that the scheme constrains their neighbours to join with them in a collectively-advantageous enterprise.

Information and economic coordination

Just as Keynesians were sceptical about the ability of free markets to keep the economy at its natural rates of output and unemployment over time, so they believed that the '**invisible hand**' was ill-suited to the task of coordinating investment across a modern economy.

For the car industry, for example, to invest in new, high-tech plant and equipment, its managers had to be confident of the future demand for their products – a guarantee provided by the government's commitment to maintain a high level of aggregate demand. But if the industry's expansion were not to be choked off by shortages of machinery and skilled workers, it required that the capital goods industry, in turn, was geared up to provide the extra machine tools needed by car producers; and that the school system was equipping school-leavers with the knowledge to use the new machinery. *Keynesians asked: how was this degree of coordination to be achieved across a complex, interdependent economy?*

Given the long *lead times* between the decision to produce and the delivery of the finished product, Keynesians doubted that price signals alone would work to coordinate the plans of different sectors. How were machine-tool makers to know that the car industry intended a major expansion? When the increase in investment started to take place, the car industry would accordingly find the machine-tool sector without the capacity to respond. While shortages would drive up the price of machine tools, thereby stimulating an increase in output, it might take months, even years, before supply fully responded to the increased demand from the car industry.

Keynes scores first in the Old Saws Test

ANTHONY HARRIS

The surge of growth just reported in Japan should have Lord Keynes cheering in his grave. Here is a recovery produced by Keynes's own method – heavy deficit spending on public works.

This is widely supposed to be impossible in the modern world: the bond market vigilantes would never allow it. But they have. Meanwhile, the French are proving Keynes's negative message: the futility of trying to balance the budget in a recession. The Commission des Comptes estimated last week that M Juppé's policies have so depressed the economy that, despite real cuts and higher taxes, revenue is falling nearly as fast as expenditure.

Sound money men, whether of the Maastricht fiscal school or just monetarists, should be coaching in the nets. Tokyo has successfully defied their rules (and proved, in passing, that devaluation does work in the right circum-stances); and the recovery breaks a sup-posedly immutable law of monetarist economics. It started *before* the surge in monetary growth which is supposed to precede any upturn. It may be too early to declare a result, though. This was only the first innings; and while two current dogmas should be dropped by the selectors, one remains doubtful.

First, the duds. The practice of fiscal Puritanism has never been as rigid as Thatcherite handbag rules suggest. The French may have forgotten it, and Gordon Brown never have learned: but Lord Lawson, and even the Maastricht draftsmen, recognised that deficits may properly rise during a recession. Where high debt precludes actual reflation, there are other ways: the US shows that growth and employment can be sus-tained even with a tight Budget given enough monetary stimulus.

Current experience, then, does not suggest a world without constraints; simply a more pragmatic approach to policymaking.

The Times, 19 June 1996

Similarly, it may take years for local schools to adjust the mix of their vocational training courses to meet the changing needs of employers like the car industry.

In other words, when there are long time lags between firms receiving price signals and actually responding with changes in production, events may have moved on – *so that by the time the supply side responses actually come, they are no longer appropriate.*

Keynesians concluded that the invisible hand was therefore likely to be incapable of coordinating the investment decisions across the economy in a way that would maximize the rate of economic growth. While the guarantee of high and stable levels of aggregate demand would undoubtedly help, Keynesians argued that governments should play a more explicit role in ensuring balanced growth.

This attitude to the functioning of the economy became influential in the early 1960s, following the apparent success of national economic planning in countries as diverse as the former Soviet Union, Japan and France.

The Keynesian supply side prescription

As we have seen, Keynesians were highly sceptical of the ability of free markets to function efficiently. They argued that the widespread existence of externalities, market failure, and the inability of the price mechanism to carry the information necessary to coordinate economic decision-making would result in sub-optimal rates of economic growth.

Persuaded by the Keynesians' diagnosis of Britain's economic ills, successive governments during the period 1945–79 concentrated their supply side efforts on three main fronts:

- attempts to plan the economy;
- taking firms into public ownership;
- government-directed investment and industrial restructuring.

Conclusions

From 1945 until 1979, macroeconomic policy in the UK followed the prescriptions of the Keynesian tradition.

In principle, demand management was used to stabilize aggregate demand at a level consistent with the natural rate of output. In practice, political pressures often resulted in governments overstimulating demand, reaping the electoral benefits of a temporarily lower rate of unemployment at the cost of higher inflation in the longer term.

While an important justification of fine-tuning was that it promoted economic growth by providing the conditions in which firms could invest with confidence, Keynesians also prescribed a raft of explicit supply side policies. These were justified on the grounds of widespread market failure. Policies included indicative planning, nationalization, and various measures, both indirect (e.g. fiscal carrots and sticks) and direct, to stimulate R&D and investment in physical and human capital.

These policies were not without their critics. **New Classical** economists attacked fine-tuning as inflationary and counterproductive, rejecting the notion that the private sector was inherently unstable and claiming that wages adjusted rapidly to changes in prices.

More significantly, they also dismissed the idea that the price mechanism was unable to coordinate economic activity and generate the optimal levels of investment, claiming instead that Britain's supply side weaknesses resulted from excessive government interference in the economy, rather than any inherent deficiency in the private sector.

New Classical economists alleged that the growth of the public sector, which took output and employment decisions on non-commercial grounds, and the increase in taxes necessary to finance the welfare state, had seriously damaged the incentives to invest.

It is to this critique of the Keynesian era and the policy recommendations of the New Classical school that we turn in Chapter 4.

KEY WORDS	
Keynesian view	Market failure
Sticky downwards	Externality
Discretionary fiscal and	Social optimum
monetary policy	Invisible hand
Fine-tuning	New Classical

Reading list

Kuehn, D.A., 'Why should the government seek to regulate the economy?', *Economics Today*, January 1994, 20–23.

Wilkinson, M., Chapters 3 and 4 in *Equity, Efficiency and Market Failure*, 2nd edn, Heinemann Educational, 1996.

Essay topics

1. Explain how the use of a reflationary fiscal policy may influence: (a) the level of aggregate demand; (b) the level of unemployment; (c) the aggregate price level. [40, 30, 30 marks]
   [University of London Examinations and Assessment Council 1994]

2. 'Keynes's solution to unemployment was higher public spending, which would add to incomes and, through the multiplier process, lead to more jobs' – *Economics Today*, September 1993.
   (a) Explain how Keynes's solution is supposed to work. [13 marks]
   (b) Are there any other solutions to the problem of unemployment? [12 marks]
   [University of Cambridge Local Examinations Syndicate 1996]

3. Explain what is meant by full employment and outline the problems of its measurement. Is stable full employment a feasible target for a government? [25 marks]
   [Northern Examinations and Assessment Board 1994]

Data Response Question

This task is based on a question set by the Welsh Joint Education Committee in 1994. Study Figures A and B before answering the questions.

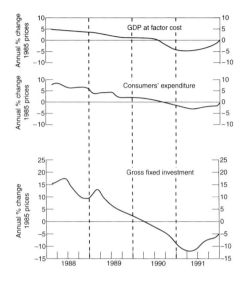

Figure A UK consumption, investment and GDP, 1988–91

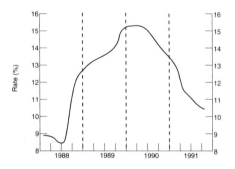

Figure B UK interest rates, 1988–91

1. Describe the trends in consumption, investment and GDP between 1988 and 1991. [4 marks]
2. (a) What do the data suggest about the relationship between GDP and investment? [3 marks]
   (b) Explain whether this relationship is the one that might be expected in economic theory. [5 marks]
3. Did the fall in interest rates during 1990 have the effect on consumption and investment that might have been expected? Give reasons for your answer. [7 marks]
4. Explain *two* possible reasons why the government increased interest rates so sharply during 1988 and 1989. [6 marks]

Chapter Four

The New Classical approach to the supply side

'We need a complete change of attitude towards the way our economy works ... to remove the constraints imposed by the tax system and by the unduly large role previously played by the government, releasing initiative and enterprise.' HM Treasury, 1979

Introduction

In the late 1970s, the policy prescriptions of the Keynesians came under increasing attack from a group of economists known as the **New Classical School**. Initially, these critics of the prevailing orthodoxy attracted most attention for their claim that excessive monetary growth was the root of the inflation then plaguing the British economy. This insistence that money – which played only a minor role in Keynesian explanations of inflation – was the key factor determining prices quickly acquired these mavericks the label 'monetarists'.

But their differences with the Keynesians were much more fundamental than the question of whether monetary, as opposed to fiscal, policy was the more powerful influence on aggregate demand. Their theories amounted to a revival, albeit with modifications and refinements, of the classical school of macroeconomics that had been ousted by the Keynesian 'revolution' in the 1930s. As their ideas became more widely known, not least as a result of the enthusiasm with which they were taken up by Mrs Thatcher's Conservative governments after 1979, the more accurate designation of the New Classical school gradually gained acceptance. The New Classical economists believed that:

- the private sector was inherently efficient, with unfettered labour and goods markets clearing quickly and the economy automatically tending to its natural rate of output;
- discretionary demand management policy, far from being necessary to stabilize aggregate demand and thereby promote investment and economic growth, had in fact been positively destabilizing.

This was because, when aggregate demand changed spontaneously, the private sector rapidly began to adapt its price and wage-fixing behaviour. Policy adjustments by the government, which inevitably

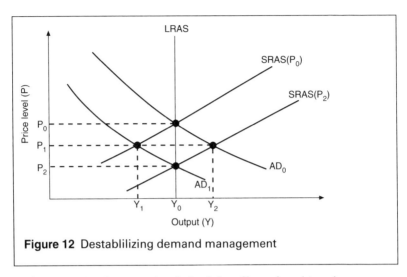

Figure 12 Destablilizing demand management

took time to implement, simply had the effect of pushing the economy further in the direction it was already moving, causing it to overshoot the natural rate of output, causing either inflation or unemployment.

For example, if aggregate demand were to fall in Figure 12 from AD_0 to AD_1, the short-run aggregate supply schedule would quickly shift down from $SRAS(P_0)$ to $SRAS(P_2)$, as lower prices fed through into lower wage settlements. If the government responded to the initial contraction in demand by relaxing fiscal and monetary policy, driving aggregate demand back to AD_0, as these lagged effects spread through the economy, the economy would slide up its new short-run aggregate supply schedule, $SRAS(P_2)$, throwing the economy back into disequilibrium just as it was recovering from the initial **demand-side 'shock'**.

Moreover, to the extent that markets did not appear to clear as smoothly as New Classical economists claimed, they argued that any sluggishness was due to the interference of government, which had injected damaging distortions into the economic system. Nationalization, state controls and regulations and high taxes were singled out for particular criticism in this regard. In contrast to the Keynesians, who had highlighted the importance of market failure as the primary source of supply side weakness in the British economy, the New Classical economists stressed the need to liberate and properly reward individual enterprise.

The rationale of New Classical supply side policies

Like Keynesians, the New Classical school faced the task of explaining why it is that some countries undertake more research and development (R&D) and invest more in physical and human capital than others, thereby reaping the benefits of faster economic growth.

In providing their answer to this conundrum, the New Classical school emphasized the importance of individual economic agents, motivated by self-interest and reacting to the incentives and sanctions provided by the economic system within which they operate. In this, the New Classical economists drew upon a long tradition, extending back to Adam Smith's famous book, *Wealth of Nations*, and revitalized by the more recent ideas of **Hayek** and the so-called **Austrian School** (see the box on page 40).

The latter stressed the vital function of competitive markets in providing people with the incentives to seek out information about profitable opportunities for production and exchange. Information concerning the most efficient methods of production and which goods are most valued by consumers will only be discovered by economic agents with a personal incentive to do so, because they expect to benefit as a consequence.

The key economic agents on the supply side of the economy are the various categories of producers – **entrepreneurs**, managers and workers – together with investors (those people who are postponing consumption by investing in productive assets) and their advisers, the financial institutions. According to the New Classical view, entrepreneurs are motivated by the expectation of profit to discover and supply products that consumers want and to use efficient production methods. The stimulus to serve consumers is best provided in competitive markets. Without the stimulus of competition, a firm has less inducement to organize its workforce efficiently, to provide its employees with incentives to work efficiently and to satisfy customers' wants.

The New Classical economists' scepticism about the ability of governments to improve economic performance by means of direct intervention is based on the argument that governments cannot obtain the requisite information about the most efficient ways of allocating resources. The market is more efficient at discovering and transmitting such information because it relies on specialists in particular market niches obtaining and using information about the kinds of goods and services demanded by consumers and about the cheapest methods of production. The economy is in a constant state of flux as changes occur in technical knowledge, in the prices of raw materials or in consumer tastes. It is also dynamic, in the sense that it continually generates new applications for technical knowledge and adapts rapidly and smoothly to changes in the forces of demand and supply, if and only if individual economic agents have the appropriate incentives. Only the market can produce 'spontaneous order', argued Hayek.

In Praise of Hayek

Like Maynard Keynes, Friedrich von Hayek achieved fame less for what he wrote than for what others said he wrote. The economic philosophy he developed over six decades, and especially during the 20 years he spent at the London School of Economics after 1931, was not, as so many now suppose, 'neo-conservatism'.

Call him instead an original thinker in the tradition of classical liberalism – perhaps the century's finest.

Much of Hayek's work is difficult; all of it is idiosyncratic. His writings seem especially peculiar to economists trained in the modern Anglo-American way, because Hayek rejected that school's paradigm: the idea of a static system in which certain stable properties (many buyers, many sellers, perfect information, homogenous goods) yield certain stable results (an optimal allocation of resources). Hayek was interested in markets and economies as systems in flux. In his scheme, sequences of events, not states of affairs, were the object of study. Anglo-American economics starts by abstracting from change and time – and is then obliged to reintroduce them, with difficulty, to make its analysis more informative. Hayek, and others of the so-called Austrian School, put change and time at the centre from the outset.

Other themes seem to follow naturally from that perspective. They recur in almost everything Hayek wrote.

The most crucial is the notion of a market as a process of discovery. Modern economies are vastly complicated. Somehow they must process immense quantities of information – concerning the tastes and incomes of consumers, the outputs and costs of production, and the myriad inter-dependencies of all of the above. The task of gathering this information, let alone making sense of it, is beyond any designing intelligence. But it is not beyond the market, which yields **'spontaneous order'** out of chaos. Hayek looked on the miracle of the invisible hand with the same delight as Adam Smith. He celebrated it anew, and made it his mission to understand it.

Source: abridged from an obituary in *The Economist,* 28 March 1992

On this view of the world, the role of government is to ensure that the laws, regulations and institutions operate so as to provide economic agents with the required incentives and information. Direct intervention by government – with the objective of determining which goods should be produced, where investment should be directed, which areas of research should be investigated or what prices should be charged – is doomed to be inefficient. Governments cannot obtain the requisite information at the right time and are pressured by special interest (or '**rent-seeking**') groups to allocate resources to satisfy their own specific interests (see also Chapter 7).

The rationale of New Classical supply side policies is thus derived directly from this view of how markets operate in allocating resources, in contrast to the comparative inefficiency of government regulation. The general aim of New Classical supply side policies is to strengthen and extend competitive market forces and to alter existing laws and regulations in order to improve the incentives for individuals to seek out productive activities.

Inspired by the New Classical school, the Conservative government that came to power in 1979 rejected the Keynesian supply side policies that it inherited and introduced a raft of new measures which included:

- privatization of public enterprises;
- deregulation of the goods and capital markets, thereby encouraging competition;
- reform of the tax and social security system to increase incentives to work and invest;
- legislative changes designed to liberalize the labour market;
- reduction in red tape and other impediments to investment and risk-taking;
- reduction in government expenditure to release more resources for the private sector;
- abolition of exchange controls and other impediments to the free movement of capital;
- increasing share ownership;
- improvements in the skills and training of the labour force;
- development of mass home ownership.

These dimensions of supply side programmes are discussed more fully in the later chapters.

Conclusions

There was certainly a 'complete change in attitude' in the 1980s towards the way the UK economy should work. We have seen that, in contrast to the Keynesian school of thought, New Classical economists believe that free markets, left to their own devices, will best allocate resources between competing ends in an efficient way. They are sceptical of the Keynesian's insistence on government intervention to strengthen the supply side. Indeed, New Classical economists typically regard attempts by the state to control private sector activity as counter-productive, blaming the UK's relatively poor postwar supply side record on excessive government interference.

Inspired by this theoretical approach to the supply side, the post-1979 Conservative governments have directed policy at 'freeing the market', by privatizing nationalized industries, rationalizing the tax and social security system, and reforming the UK's notoriously inflexible labour market.

The remaining chapters of this book consider the operation and performance of recent supply side policies in the most important areas, as well as considering wider international supply side measures.

KEY WORDS

New Classical School   Austrian School
Demand-side shock   Entrepeneurs
Hayek   Rent-seeking

Reading list
Smith, D., Chapters 1, 6 and 7 in *Mrs Thatcher's Economics: Her Legacy*, 2nd edn, Heinemann Educational, 1992.
Willets, D., Chapters 6 and 9 in *Modern Conservatism*, Penguin, 1992.

Essay topics
1. (a) Explain what is meant by the 'natural rate of unemployment' (also known as NAIRU). [30 marks]
   (b) Evaluate the effects of demand side and supply side policies on the NAIRU. [70 marks]
   [University of London Examinations and Assessment Council 1995]
2. (a) Monetarists and supply side economists believe that an economy has a natural rate of unemployment. (i) What is the natural rate of unemployment? (ii) What factors determine whether the natural rate of unemployment in an economy is likely to be high or low. [5, 7 marks]
   (b) Assess the significance of the 'natural rate of unemployment hypothesis' for the conduct of economic policy. [13 marks]
   [Associated Examining Board 1995]
3. (a) What is the economic rationale underlying a government

'spending its way out of a recession'? [10 marks]
(b) To what extent is its ability to do so limited? [15 marks]
[University of Oxford Delegacy of Local Examinations 1995]
4. Explain what constitutes macroeconomic policy. Outline the broad changes that British macroeconomic policy has undergone since the 1970s, and evaluate the success of current measures. [25 marks]
[Northern Examinations and Assessment Board 1994]
5. Is 'full employment' any longer a realistic macroeconomic policy objective? [25 marks]
[Oxford & Cambridge Schools Examination Board 1996]

Data Response Question
This task is based on a question set by the Associated Examining Board in 1994. Read the extract, which is adapted from an article by John Grieve-Smith, published in *The Observer* in November 1991. Then answer the questions.

One-way street to an economic dead-end

Despite the undoubted success of Keynesian demand management in achieving full employment for the first 25 years after the Second World War, a generation has grown up that is in danger of adopting the inter-war attitude of fatalistic acceptance of mass unemployment.

This is partly attributable to the growth of the extreme doctrines of market economics associated with Hayek and Friedman, and which provided the intellectual content of Thatcherism, denying the ability of, or need for, governments to influence the economy.

In their extreme form, these ideas influenced, but never captured, finance ministries and central banks. Although 'demand management' became unfashionable, in practice it remained inescapable. Any central bank or government has to take decisions continually on monetary policy, public expenditure and taxation, which affect demand. The truth is not that demand management has been dropped; but since the 1970s, the emphasis has shifted almost exclusively towards keeping demand down to fight inflation. The growth of 'one-way demand management' – a wayward offspring of the Keynesian revolution – is hindering discussion on how to get out of the recession.

The tragedy of one-way economics is that in the long run it makes high unemployment inevitable. After every downturn in the economic cycle, with its closures and bankruptcies, we are left with the ability to employ only a proportion of the labour force. Hence, when

---

the economy does recover, inflation re-emerges at a relatively high level of unemployment. The Lawson boom was a vivid illustration of this. At the same time the balance of trade becomes more precarious as our manufacturing base contracts.

Given the problems of interest rate policy, the stimulus can only come from fiscal rather than monetary policy. There has, however, been a deafening silence about the use of such measures from all parts of the political spectrum. While one-way demand management holds sway, it is regarded as financially 'responsible' only to depress the economy, not to stimulate it.

Expansionary policies will however be possible only if we devise alternative means of tackling inflation. At present any recovery, whether spontaneous or government-induced, is liable to lead to a renewed wage-price spiral, unless there is a crucial change in present pay bargaining methods. The problem is that pay settlements that are acceptable to the two negotiating parties on their own, tend to be inflationary for the economy as a whole.

The persistence of mass unemployment in the 1990s would not only cause immense human suffering, but could once again pose a threat to European democracy, as it did in the 1930s.

1. Distinguish between monetary and fiscal policy. [3 marks]
2. Explain the difference between 'one-way demand management' and conventional Keynesian demand management. [5 marks]
3. Using the passage and your knowledge of economics, explain the mechanisms by which:
   (a) one-way demand management might lead to persistent unemployment, to inflation and to balance of payments problems; [7 marks]
   (b) expansionary policies might lead to a wage-price spiral. [5 marks]

Chapter Five

Labour market reform

'Britain is the most attractive country among all European locations for the production of cars ... This results from the structural reforms initiated by Margaret Thatcher in the early 1980s, the most significant being the rearrangement of industrial relations between companies and trade unions.' Bernd Pischetsrieder, Chairman of BMW

Introduction

A central plank of the Conservative administrations' supply side pro-gramme after 1979 was reform of the labour market. It is important to note that many of the tax and social security policies were intended to work through the labour market:

- Reductions in employers' national insurance contributions (NICs) reduce the cost of labour to employers, encouraging them to expand employment and thus increasing the **natural rate of output**.
- Income tax cuts and reductions in social security benefits increase the incentive to work, thereby increasing the supply of labour at any given wage rate and so increasing the natural rate of output.

The labour market reforms discussed in this chapter, however, relate to measures that impact directly on the labour market in the first instance – for example, changes to the laws on collective wage bar-gaining by trade unions.

Trade unions and the supply side

The Conservative governments charged trade unions with inhibiting the flexible operation of the labour market by preventing necessary downwards adjustments in wages, and thereby prolonging the period during which **deflationary shocks** to the economy depress output below its natural rate – and correspondingly push unemployment above its natural rate.

In other words, in terms of the aggregate supply and demand (AS–AD) model, trade unions are accused of extending the length of the short run, by slowing down the speed with which wages and prices adjust to slumps in AD so that the economy returns to its natural rate of output more slowly than would otherwise be the case.

Introducing the role of trade unions into the AS–AD model in this way suggests there is likely to be an important asymmetry in the way the economy adjusts to changes in AD.

- Following a fall in AD, rational behaviour by monopolistic trade unions will tend to drag out the adjustment process, extending the period during which the economy languishes below its natural rate of output.
- Conversely, an increase in AD is likely to have only a transitory effect on output and employment as trade unions immediately seek to bargain for wage increases to compensate for any rise in prices.

The implication is that, by distorting the functioning of the supply side in this fashion, *the presence of trade unions will tend to lower the average long-run rate of output and raise the average long-run rate of unemployment.* This is because cyclical fluctuations in AD will boost prices and wages, rather than output and employment, in an upswing, but depress output below its natural rate and increase unemployment in recession, having only a muted effect on prices and wages.

Trade union legislation

Since 1979, a series of statutes has placed restrictions on trade union activity, in order, according to a Treasury statement in 1986, to:

> '*reduce the monopoly power of the trade unions* ... [and so] ... *create a climate in which realistic pay bargaining and acceptance of flexible working practices become the norm.*'

The government has targeted two aspects of trade unions in particular: first, their ability to undertake strike action; and secondly, their right to enforce a 'closed shop' (an arrangement whereby all employees within a company must belong to a recognized trade union – a labour-supply monopoly).

- The Employment Act 1980 made secondary picketing illegal.
- The Employment Act 1982 specified that a lawful trade dispute must 'wholly or mainly' relate to employment matters, in an attempt to prevent political strikes.
- The Trade Union Act 1984 required industrial action to be formally approved in advance by the union members concerned in a secret ballot.
- The Employment Act 1988 gave union members the right not to be disciplined by their union for failing to take part in industrial action, further weakening a union's ability to mobilize an effective strike.

- The Employment Act 1990 made it unlawful to deny people a job on the grounds that they are not union members.
- The Trade Union and Labour Relations (Consolidation) Act 1992 specified details of union ballots and the regulation of unions' financial affairs. It further stated the conditions for a union to expel or discipline a member and made it unlawful for employers to penalize workers for joining or refusing to join a union.
- The Trade Union Reform and Employment Rights Act 1993 extended the provisions of the 1992 Act – effectively ending the closed shop, requiring employers to obtain workers' written permission before union dues could be deducted from their pay packets, and requiring all union ballots to be postal.

The results of this legislative onslaught on the trade union movement have been profound. It is difficult to disentangle the effects of the new laws (which have tended to reduce the benefits of union membership) from those resulting from structural economic change (which have altered the composition of the employed labour force, creating female, part-time jobs at the expense of traditional, full-time manual employment). However, as Figure 13 shows, between 1979 and 1995 **union density** has fallen dramatically.

> **Union density** is defined as the percentage of employed workers eligible for membership of a trade union who actually exercise this right and join a union.

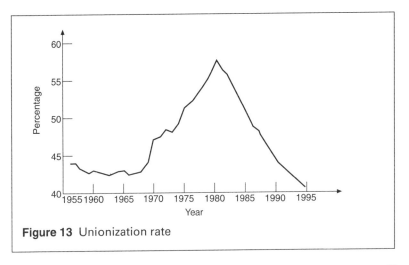

Figure 13 Unionization rate

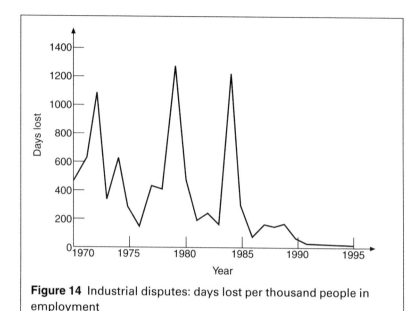

Figure 14 Industrial disputes: days lost per thousand people in employment

Although Conservative governments never suggested that they actively sought this outcome, the decline in union membership has nevertheless been at least partially influenced by the more hostile legislative environment and *has played a major part in altering the balance of power in the industrial relations arena.*

A less controversial indicator of the success of the government's new legal framework for wage bargaining has been the marked fall in the number of days lost through industrial disputes, as shown by Figure 14. Although there was a sudden surge in days lost during the protracted and highly divisive miners' strike of 1984–85, the underlying trend since 1979 appears to have been firmly downwards.

Labour mobility and the natural rate of unemployment

In addition to reducing the monopoly power of trade unions and removing legislative obstacles, the objective 'improving the flexibility of the labour market' has also included measures to promote both occupational and geographical **labour mobility.**

These policies have been inspired by the apparent increase in the *natural rate of unemployment* in the economy over the last 25 years. As we saw in Chapter 3, the natural rate of unemployment is the rate of unemployment consistent with equilibrium in the labour market; that is, with the supply of labour equal to the demand for labour.

- ● Occupational mobility

Although there are sound supply side reasons for investing resources in the training and education of all workers – in order to improve their productivity – the Conservatives' training policies have been primarily directed at the long-term unemployed, with the aim of equipping the unemployed with the appropriate skills they need to find work.

Youth Training Schemes and Job Training Schemes for young workers date back to the early 1980s. 'Restart' and similar training and re-skilling programmes targeted at the unemployed, with varying degrees of success, have also proved a major element in the government's response to persistent mismatches of supply and demand in the labour market.

- ● Geographical mobility

One of the major impediments to job mobility from the northern regions of high unemployment to the relatively more prosperous South East of England is the higher cost of private housing in the south. Approximately 70 per cent of families now live in their own homes, forcing them to buy and sell if they are to take jobs in other regions.

Although the slump in the housing market since 1988 has hit the South East hardest, reducing the size of the 'north–south' price differential, house prices in the South East still remain an average of 50 per cent higher than those in the northern regions. In addition, for approximately 1.5 million households there is the problem of **negative equity** which also prevents them from moving, even though building societies and banks have come up with ingenious schemes to help people around this problem.

For those in rented accommodation, long waiting lists make it very difficult to obtain council housing in a new area. The setting up of a Tenants' Exchange Scheme and a National Mobility Office are designed to assist geographical mobility, but it remains restricted owing to high house prices in the South East, cuts in local authority housing programmes, and the continued absence of a significant private rented sector.

Wages councils and minimum wages

In many non-unionized sectors of the economy, earlier governments had previously established 'wages councils' to enforce minimum wages, in the belief that employers would otherwise exploit their relative bargaining power by paying unacceptably low wages.

The Conservative government argued that such agencies produced similar distortions to trade unions, tending to raise minimum wages in line with prices, but responding slowly to downward pressure on prices and company profits during recessionary periods.

For this reason, the Conservative government abolished wage councils in August 1993. With the abolition of wages councils the UK became the only European Union country without any formal or informal system of minimum wages.

Since these changes, a recent survey has compared women who were employed in wages council industries before and after the abolition with those who were employed in non-wages council industries. It was found that, although wages had fallen, albeit slowly, the relative employment rates of women who used to work in wages council sectors had not changed much.

The issue of a national, as opposed to a sectoral, minimum wage leapt on to the political agenda in late 1991, during the negotiations that led up to the European Union's Maastricht Summit. The UK refused to sign the **Social Chapter**, arguing that the raft of social rights and benefits embodied in it would reintroduce obstacles to labour market flexibility and strengthen the position of trade unions. However, the implications of the Social Chapter have begun to be introduced through the 'back door' as a number of UK multinationals have offered the same packages to their UK workforces as they do to their continental European workforces.

Worst of the elements of the Social Chapter was considered to be the notion of a national minimum wage which was viewed as a massive labour market rigidity.

The following are arguments *in favour* of such a minimum wage:

- It would help to reduce poverty.
- By paying a minimum wage employers would be forced to become more efficient, investing in better levels of technology.
- There would be less demand for state benefits.
- Government tax revenue would increase.

There are also arguments *against* a national minimum wage:

- There would be an increase in unemployment.
- Higher wages for low paid workers would encourage other workers to demand higher wages to protect their differential salary conditions.
- Higher wages for public sector workers would put pressure on government finances.
- Higher wage bills would be passed on to consumers through higher prices.

The extent to which the costs and benefits from a minimum wage accrue to society depends upon the level at which the minimum wage is set. However, there is some evidence from applied analysis studies in the United States to suggest that minimum wages are popular with the public, improve the incentives to enter the job market, and do not seem to have a detrimental effect on jobs.

Conclusions

A flexible, efficient labour force is clearly crucial for a successful supply side. There is little doubt that, before 1979, the British labour market was excessively rigid, plagued by poor industrial relations, and subject to unrealistic attitudes to pay and performance. The trade union reforms undertaken by the Conservative administrations, initially against strong opposition from the labour movement, have proved electorally popular. While the UK may yet sign up for the EU's Social Chapter sometime in the future, thus extending trade union powers in certain limited areas, it seems likely that the balance of industrial power between employers and unions has changed permanently.

In other respects, Conservative governments have introduced useful schemes to promote occupational and geographical mobility, aimed at reducing the natural rate of unemployment, but these appear to have been swamped by a sharp increase in **structural unemployment**. Moreover, the data presented in Chapter 3 and above on skill shortages and the poor standard of training and education suggest that the UK still faces serious, and as yet unresolved, problems in terms of the quality of its labour force.

KEY WORDS

Natural rate of unemployment	Labour mobility
Deflationary shocks	Wages councils
Union density	Social Chapter
	Structural unemployment

Reading list

Simpson, L., and Paterson, I., *The UK Labour Market*, Heinemann Educational, 1995.

Essay topics

1. (a) Outline and explain the main changes in unemployment that have occurred in the UK during the last 10 years. [12 marks]
   (b) Evaluate the extent to which government policies have influenced the level of unemployment. [13 marks]
   [Associated Examining Board 1996]

2. (a) Use the concept of opportunity cost to explain why a production possibility frontier is usually drawn as a curve. [15 marks]
   (b) How might imperfections in the labour market prevent the economy from moving on to the production possibility curve? [10 marks]
   [University of Cambridge Local Examinations Syndicate 1996]

3. Explain and discuss the following:
   (a) part-time workers often being paid at an hourly rate less than full-time workers; [8 marks]
   (b) firms paying overtime rates that are greater than normal wage rates; [8 marks]
   (c) government subsidising employers who take on additional workers from those who have been unemployed for at least six months. [9 marks]
   [University of Oxford Delegacy of Local Examinations 1995]

4. In 1984 over 27 million working days were lost in industrial stoppages. By 1994 the number had fallen to 280 thousand, the lowest ever recorded. Account for the reduction. [25 marks]
   [Oxford & Cambridge Schools Examination Board 1996]

5. (a) What do you understand by 'supply side policies'? [20 marks]
   (b) How might supply side policies be used to reduce the level of unemployment? [50 marks]
   (c) Examine the limitations of using supply side policies as a means of reducing the level of unemployment. [30 marks]
   [University of London Examinations and Assessment Council 1995]

Data Response Question

This task is based on a question set by the Associated Examining Board in 1996. Read the article, which is adapted from pieces in *The Economist* of 16 April and 3 September 1994, together with Figure A which is adapted from *Fiscal Studies* in August 1991. Then answer the questions.

Minimum wages

Britain differs from most European Union countries and from America in having no statutory minimum wage.

Supporters of minimum wages say that they are needed to combat poverty among the low-paid. On the face of it, they would seem to help a significant number of workers. Around 5 per cent of full-time jobs pay less than £3.40 an hour before tax; more than 10 per cent of workers earn less than £4. Nearly 17 per cent of women get less than £4 an hour, compared with less than 8 per cent of men. One probably cleans your office. Another pulls your pint.

There is, though, an obvious objection to a minimum wage. It forces companies to pay more for their lowest-cost staff, which in theory should prompt them to shed jobs among the unskilled and the young. And some fear that minimum wages at the bottom then tempt higher-paid workers to push for higher pay for themselves, to restore wage differentials; that costs jobs further up the pay scales and may cause inflation.

The theory is probably right. By and large, empirical studies of the effects of minimum wages – most of which are based on American evidence – suggest that they do increase unemployment, especially among young people. But they do so at most only modestly; and the evidence is far from overwhelming.

Recent research suggests that, in certain circumstances, labour-market rigidities may prevent minimum wages from harming employment. David Card and Paul Krueger, two Princeton economists, looked at the effect, in 1992, of New Jersey raising its minimum wage from $4.25 to $5.05 an hour, while neighbouring Pennsylvania stuck to $4.25. They found that employment in the fast-food industry grew by 13 per cent more in New Jersey than it did in Pennsylvania.

This body of research shows that, in particular industries at particular times, a minimum wage might not destroy jobs. It could entice someone who lived on welfare to take a job. Better-paid employees might work harder and change jobs less frequently, while employers might invest more in their training.

This latest research does not convince everyone. Molly Meacher, a British economist, claimed that a national minimum wage would either have to be set at such a low level that it would be a mere token, or at a high enough level so that – as in France and Spain – it harmed employment. Among French workers aged under 26, one in four is out of a job. Economic growth in both France and Spain was under half that of Britain in 1993–94.

A minimum wage might also overcome the problem of the

'poverty trap' which discourages some of the unemployed from taking jobs, but job losses would limit the impact of minimum wages on poverty. Increased wages for some would come at the cost of joblessness for others. And, that aside, there is another good reason for not wanting a minimum wage. Often, the low-paid are not poor: according to the Institute for Fiscal Studies, a think-tank, a minimum wage would benefit mainly the wives of working husbands and young people living at home. The poor, more likely, are those who are not working at all. In families with dependent children where the husband is out of a job, only 1 per cent of wives work. Fewer than half of all lone mothers are employed.

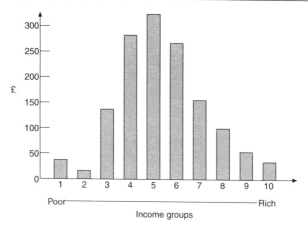

Figure A Average annual gain per household from a minimum wage of £3.50 per hour

In Figure A, income group 1 represents the poorest 10 per cent of households in the UK.

1. Explain what is meant by a 'statutory minimum wage'. [2 marks]
2. Using economic analysis, explain why 'more than 10 per cent of (full-time) workers earn less than £4 (an hour)'. [4 marks]
3. Using a diagram, explain how the introduction of a minimum wage could raise the wages of low-paid workers. [4 marks]
4. Discuss the effects that the introduction of a minimum wage might have on poverty in the UK. [6 marks]
5. The information provided shows that the outcome of the introduction of a minimum wage is disputed. Discuss the effects such an introduction might have on employment and inflation in the UK economy. [9 marks]

Chapter Six
Taxation and social security

'In this world nothing can be said to be certain, except death and taxes.' Benjamin Franklin

Introduction
Changes in the inherited structure of taxes and social security have been a key theme of Conservative administrations since 1979. As noted in Chapter 4, previous governments had tended to lay great stress on the need to fine tune aggregate demand – that is, to maintain aggregate demand at a level that kept the economy at full employment – by altering tax rates with little regard to the indirect effects on the supply side.

To the extent that other considerations were weighed in the balance, these were primarily concerned with social issues of equity and income distribution, rather than with the impact of tax and social security on the supply side of the economy.

This approach was overturned by the incoming Conservative government in 1979. It pledged itself to reducing direct taxes on income and profit – preferably by first reducing government spending, but if necessary by increasing indirect taxes on spending such as VAT and customs and excise duties. In announcing his first budget, the then Chancellor of the Exchequer, Sir Geoffrey Howe, claimed:

'Our new economic strategy is built around our tax proposals. Income tax now takes a high proportion of even modest incomes. This gives rise to ... the sapping of effort and initiative ... and bears a considerable responsibility for industry's lack of competitiveness.'

The effect of taxes and social security on incentives
The effect of taxes and social security on the incentive to work can be easily analysed using the simple tools of microeconomics. The important point in analysing the supply of labour is to recognize that the decision by a worker to supply work is equivalent to the decision to give up leisure. Thus, the appropriate analysis is to consider the choice between income and leisure – every hour of leisure taken is an hour of income sacrificed.

An increase in the wage rate that could arise through a reduction in taxes will lead to two effects – a **substitution** and an **income effect**.

A reduction in taxes means that an individual will receive a greater amount of income per hour. Each hour of leisure (assuming it to be a normal good) an individual chooses is therefore more expensive in terms of income foregone, so there will be a *substitution* away from leisure. However, along with the substitution effect there will also be an income effect. The increase in wages that an individual receives through a tax reduction allows the individual to obtain more of *both* leisure *and* work.

Therefore, the impact of a reduction in taxes on whether an individual takes more leisure – offers fewer hours of work to the labour market – is the sum of these two effects. It is possible to get a whole range of possible outcomes.

- If the reduction in taxes leads to a substitution effect away from leisure that exceeds the income effect towards leisure, then the individual will supply more hours of work to the labour market following a tax reduction.
- On the other hand, it is possible that following a tax reduction the substitution effect away from leisure is less than the income effect of taking more leisure, and the overall effect following a tax reduction is for the individual to take more leisure time, offering fewer hours of work to the labour market.

In the case of social security benefits, there will be some individuals who are currently offering hours to the labour market. A rise in benefits may lead to them maximizing their welfare by withdrawing themselves from the labour market, preferring to be unemployed where their income (benefits) now exceeds their old level of benefit payment plus their income from working. It follows that a reduction in unemployment-related benefits will tend to increase the number of hours offered for work.

The Laffer curve

Arguing that tax and social security cuts are necessary to strengthen the supply side of the economy poses an awkward policy problem. Because the number of unemployed drawing social security is small relative to the number of taxpayers, any concerted supply side initiative is likely to result in much deeper falls in tax revenues than there are offsetting savings in social security outlays.

However, in the mid-1970s, Professor Arthur Laffer offered a solution to this apparent conflict between supply side objectives and prudent fiscal policy. He pointed out that there is logically a direct relationship between the rate of taxation and the amount of revenue raised, as demonstrated in Figure 15.

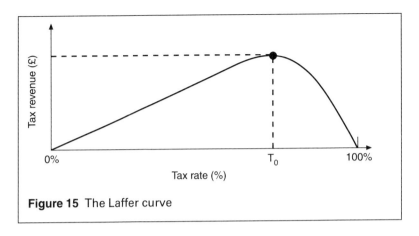

Figure 15 The Laffer curve

At a tax rate of 0 per cent, revenue will clearly be zero. At a tax rate of 100 per cent, revenue will again be zero since there is no incentive to work in a taxable activity. Between these two extremes, therefore, there will be a function relating the amount of tax revenue to the tax rate which will be positive, at some point reaching a maximum – in this case at tax rate T_0. In other words, the tax revenue function will follow the bell shape of the so-called **Laffer curve**.

Laffer was not the first to spot this relationship, as the following quotation from Adam Smith's *Wealth of Nations* suggests:

> *'High taxes, sometimes by diminishing the consumption of the taxed commodities, and sometimes by encouraging smuggling, frequently afford a smaller revenue than what might be drawn from more moderate taxes.'*

Laffer's contribution, however, was to provide an alternative explanation for a possible inverse relationship between tax rates and tax revenue, based on the effects of high taxes on the incentive to produce, rather than their tendency to depress consumption or encourage dishonest tax evasion.

This struck a sympathetic chord with many New Classical economists. They saw that, provided the government inherits tax rates that are above T_0 in Figure 15, it need not delay tax cuts for fear of running a budget deficit. This is because a cut in tax rates will not only stimulate the supply side of the economy, but – by more than proportionately boosting income – also increase tax revenue.

It was the belief that US tax rates – which were much lower than those then prevailing in Europe – were above T_0 that encouraged the incoming Reagan administration to cut income tax rates heavily between 1981and 1983 in the USA. In the event, a huge budget deficit emerged, although supporters of the Reagan tax cuts argue that this was primarily the result of a failure to control federal spending during the 1980s, rather than the depressing effect of the tax cuts on federal revenue.

In the UK, for certain sectors of the population, it was generally recognized that tax rates were above T_0. In 1979, for example, the top marginal rate of income tax was a staggering 98 per cent – comprising a tax rate of 83 per cent, plus a 15 per cent 'unearned' income surcharge for income derived from, for example, shares or property. Unsurprisingly, many wealthy individuals chose to live abroad as 'tax exiles', rather than pay such penal rates.

Significantly, as the top rates of tax in the UK have fallen below those in continental Europe, the phenomenon of rock stars commuting to London from their homes in Switzerland has ended and the share of tax revenues collected from the richest 5 per cent of the population has increased – as the Laffer curve predicts.

For the vast majority of taxpayers, however, the Conservative government was unconvinced by the argument that tax rates were above T_0. Tax cuts for average earners have been introduced slowly over

"Er... plus VAT, sir"

successive parliaments, with the Treasury reducing taxes by only what its current finances would allow – rather than risking deeper cuts in the hope of a spontaneous, supply-side-induced increase in income and tax revenues.

Tax policy between 1979 and 1995

Between 1979and 1995, Conservative administrations introduced seventeen budgets, a high proportion of which involved significant reductions in direct taxes (the exception was in 1981). However, there were major changes in indirect taxation.

As we have seen, the net incentive effect of tax cuts on households depends upon (a) the size of the (positive) substitution effect, and (b) the size of the (negative) income effect. Bearing these factors in mind, we can now assess the supply side contribution of recent tax changes as they have affected households.

In 1979, the marginal rate of income tax paid by top income earners was 83 per cent, or 98 per cent for unearned income from investments. In the period to 1996 this top rate was cut to 40 per cent, one of the lowest top rates in the European Union. The basic rate was similarly cut from an inherited rate of 33 per cent to 24 per cent, with the first £3500 at 20 per cent, and all other marginal income tax rates were abolished. The rate of VAT was sharply increased from 8 per cent in 1979 to 17.5 per cent in two jumps. Overall, therefore, it appears that the structure of income tax has become much less **progressive**, which may have improved incentives to work.

However, the situation is complicated by other factors. For example, employees' national insurance contributions (NICs) were increased from 6.5 per cent to 9 per cent over the same period. Since NICs are another tax – albeit one that is 'earmarked' for a specific purpose, which is financing social security payments to the old, sick and unemployed – *this increase means that for many income taxpayers, the reduction in their marginal tax rates was less than the cuts in income tax rates would suggest.*

Thus, while the **marginal rates of tax** faced by workers have fallen since 1979, the **average rate of tax** has actually increased slightly – despite political

rhetoric to the contrary in line with the government's declared commitment to reduce the burden of taxation.

This effect has been primarily due to **fiscal drag** – the process by which the average tax burden automatically rises during a period of economic growth.

Under the so-called **Rooker–Wise amendment**, tax allowances and bands in the UK are indexed to the retail price index, so that they are raised at each budget in line with inflation. They are not increased, however, as real incomes grow. Real income growth of roughly 3 per cent a year would have increased average earnings to £15 000 by 1992. Without any change to the tax structure, the average tax rate would have automatically increased to 16.7 per cent. It is primarily through this mechanism that the average tax rate has increased slightly in the UK.

The Community Charge

The Community Charge, or 'poll tax', is worthy of mention, as it represented the high-water mark of the New Classical tax revolution. In terms of its impact on incentives, a lump-sum tax that is unrelated to ability to pay is the ideal way of raising government revenue. For a lump-sum tax, the marginal rate of tax is 0 per cent, hence it creates no disincentive to work.

In April 1990, the government replaced the former system of domestic rates. Under this system households had paid an annual local tax related to the value of their housing – and hence, indirectly, to their wealth and income. Rates were replaced by a lump-sum **Community Charge**. Each adult within a council district was required to pay the same amount, although there was some help for the poorest individuals through the social security system.

Regardless of its elegance in supply side terms, however, the poll tax violated an important principle of taxation, namely that the system be perceived as **equitable**. In the event, the notion that a duke should pay the same local tax as his chauffeur led to a massive, and at times violent, public outcry against the system. The government quickly backed down, and in 1993 a new **Council Tax** was introduced to replace the Community Charge. Like the rates, the Council Tax is related to the value of an individual's property.

The public's rejection of the poll tax highlights the political difficulties of supply side reform in the emotive area of personal taxation.

The reform of social security

As we have seen, social security benefits also affect incentives to work, creating – through their interaction with the tax system – anomalies such as the **unemployment trap** and the **poverty trap**.

- The *unemployment trap* refers to the situation in which an individual has a higher disposable income when unemployed than if he or she worked, owing to the payment of taxes on earned income and the withdrawal of benefits. In other words, there is a positive financial *disincentive to seek work*.

The extent of this disincentive is captured by the so-called **replacement ratio**, which is defined as the ratio of total benefits while unemployed to disposable income while in work. For an unskilled worker with dependent partner and school-aged children, total unemployment-related benefits may be high relative to the disposable income that could be expected from work, resulting in a replacement ratio that may be close to, or even above, unity.

For example, imagine that weekly benefits while unemployed are £100. If the highest wage that the worker can command, net of tax, is only £120, then the replacement ratio is 100/120, or 84 per cent. When replacement ratios are high, it is easy to see why people may be deterred from working, thereby reducing the supply of labour and weakening the supply side of the economy. In our example, the unfortunate individual is *effectively* being invited to work for a mere £20 a week, so it would hardly be surprising if he or she chose leisure over full-time employment.

- The *poverty trap* is closely related to the unemployment trap, operating in a similar way for individuals on low incomes.

Because low earnings are supplemented by means-tested, or income-related, benefits – such as free school meals, free healthcare, welfare payments, etc. – a badly-designed system can twice penalize workers who take higher paying jobs.

First they are denied continued access to a means-tested benefit they previously enjoyed. Secondly, the extra income is taxed at an increasing marginal rate. In extreme cases, the overall effect can be to reduce disposable income, including non-monetary benefits, so deterring workers from seeking better-paid positions.

Conclusions

Many individuals resent paying taxes because they perceive them as taking far too much of their income. Since 1979, Conservative administrations have stressed the role of tax and social security reform in order to promote incentives to work and invest. This emphasis is, of course, partly derived from wider political objectives of promoting individual freedom and responsibility, rather than allowing people to rely passively on a paternalist welfare state. Nevertheless, the government has expected major economic dividends from the restructuring of taxes and social security in terms of a revitalized supply side.

We have seen that economic theory suggests that such reforms, by altering the opportunity cost of leisure, can have two offsetting effects:

- a positive substitution effect, whereby workers substitute work for leisure; and
- a negative income effect.

Whether tax and social security reforms are successful depends, in part, on which of these two effects is the stronger.

Theory does indicate, however, that it is marginal rates of tax that are most relevant for determining the size of the substitution effect and average rates of income tax that primarily determine the size of the income effect.

To the extent that the reforms introduced by the Conservative government have reduced marginal rates of tax, without having much impact on the overall burden of taxation, they have probably had a positive effect on incentives.

KEY WORDS

Substitution effect	Rooker–Wise amendment
Income effect	Community Charge
Laffer curve	Equitable
Progressive tax	Council Tax
Marginal tax rate	Unemployment trap
Average tax rate	Poverty trap
Fiscal drag	Replacement ratio

Reading list

Grant, S., Chapter 5 in *UK Fiscal Policy*, Heinemann Educational, 1994.

National Institute of Economic and Social Research, Chapter 4 in *The UK Economy*, 3rd edn, Heinemann Educational, 1995.

Wilkinson, M., *Equity, Efficiency and Market Failure*, 2nd edn, Heinemann Educational, 1997.

Essay topics

1. (a) Why do governments levy taxes? [12 marks]
   (b) Discuss the view that the UK government should further reduce the burden of direct taxation and recover the lost revenue by imposing substantial increases in indirect taxation. [13 marks]
   [Associated Examining Board 1995]
2. (a) Distinguish between direct and indirect taxation, and give examples of each. [10 marks]
   (b) What theoretical arguments exist to justify a movement from direct to indirect taxation? [15 marks]
   [Oxford & Cambridge Schools Examination Board 1995]
3. (a) Outline the various supply side policies that have been introduced in the UK during recent years. [10 marks]
   (b) Discuss the extent to which these supply side reforms have influenced the performance of the economy. [15 marks]
   [Associated Examining Board 1993]

Data Response Question

This task is based on a question set by the University of London Examinations and Assessment Council in 1996. Study the five charts of information about the UK economy in Figures A–E and, using your knowledge of economics, answer the questions below.

1. Explain one factor that might account for the trend in public expenditure as a percentage of GDP since 1989. [3 marks]
2. (a) Why might you expect there to be a relationship between changes in real GDP and changes in the PSBR?
   (b) To what extent do the data in Figures B and C suggest that such a relationship existed between 1985 and 1993? [6 marks]
3. How does Figure D illustrate any *three* objectives of public expenditure? [6 marks]
4. Examine the likely economic effects of the changes in the relative importance of sources of government revenue on (i) incentives to work and (ii) the distribution of income. [6, 4 marks]

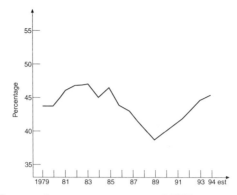

Figure A Public spending as a percentage of GDP

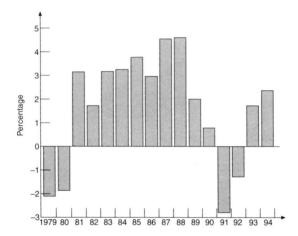

Figure B UK growth as annual percentage change in real GDP

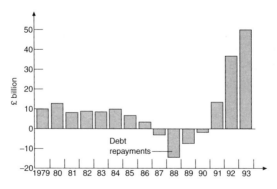

Figure C Public sector borrowing requirements (PSBR), excluding privatization proceeds

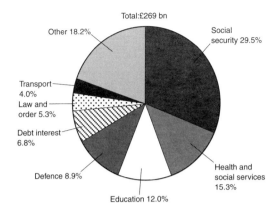

Figure D Public expenditure 1992/93
Source: *The Economist,* 4 September 1993

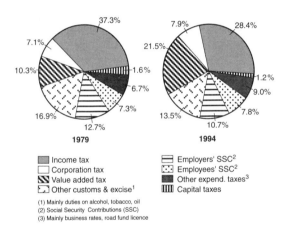

▨ Income tax	☰ Employers' SSC[2]
☐ Corporation tax	⣿ Employees' SSC[2]
▧ Value added tax	■ Other expend. taxes[3]
⣿ Other customs & excise[1]	▥ Capital taxes

(1) Mainly duties on alcohol, tobacco, oil
(2) Social Security Contributions (SSC)
(3) Mainly business rates, road fund licence

Figure E Central government's tax receipts
Source: *Dataset,* 1995

Chapter Seven

Privatization

'Privatization is a key element of the government's economic strategy ... Our main objective is to promote competition and increase efficiency.' John Moore, Financial Secretary to the Treasury, 1983

Introduction

Privatization was a central plank of the supply side strategy pursued by Conservative administrations since 1979. Ironically, however, the government did not take power in 1979 with the idea of privatizing more than a handful of state-run companies. Initially, it believed that public hostility to the idea of 'selling off the family silver' and creating private monopolies out of **nationalized industries** would limit the scope of privatization to a small number of enterprises, for example the National Freight Corporation, for which there was little rationale for public ownership.

In the event, the early privatizations proved surprisingly popular, encouraging the government to raise its sights until, eventually, giant corporations like British Telecom, British Gas and the electricity and water industries were sold off.

Table 6 lists some major privatizations to date. In total, the government sold almost £50 billion of state assets over the period 1979–96.

Although there were important supply side arguments advanced in defence of privatization, there is little doubt that other considerations played a supporting role.

- Privatization fitted with the broader political objective of widening private share ownership, thereby increasing the proportion of the electorate that had a vested interest in Conservative, rather than Labour, economic policies.
- Under British public sector accounting conventions, privatization proceeds reduce public spending. The logic is that, since capital spending in nationalized industries adds to the public expenditure totals, the sale of such public investments should reduce spending totals in a mirror-image fashion.

So long as the government was able to maintain a continuous flow

Table 6 Major British privatizations

Enterprise privatized	Year(s)
British Aerospace	1980–86
Cable and Wireless	1981–85
Associated British Ports	1983–84
Austin–Rover	1984–88
British Telecom	1984–91
Sealink	1984
National Bus Company	1986
British Gas	1986
Rolls Royce	1987
British Airports Authority	1987
British Airways	1987
British Steel	1988–89
Water Boards	1989–90
Electricity Distributors	1990
Electricity Generators	1991
British Coal	1994
Railtrack (British Rail)	1995–96
British Energy	1996

Source: HM Treasury, *Financial Statistics* (CSO)

of privatization proceeds into the Exchequer's coffers, it could use the revenues to reduce taxes.

Privatization and efficiency

While ideological and political factors have certainly influenced the privatization programme since 1979, privatization was aimed primarily at strengthening the performance of the supply side of the economy.

Ministers argued that, under public control, nationalized industries had no incentive to cut costs and respond to changing patterns of consumer demand. Since many nationalized industries enjoyed considerable monopoly power, they could easily achieve the crude financial objectives imposed on them by successive governments – such as achieving a specified rate of return on capital investment – by manipulating their prices, rather than by cutting overmanning and producing more efficiently.

Nationalized industries in the 1970s were characterized by considerable 'X-inefficiency' (that is, bureaucratic waste), overmanning and ill-directed investment. Productivity growth in the nationalized sector lagged well behind that in the private sector, and many enterprises made heavy financial losses which absorbed huge amounts of taxpayers' money. To the general public both at home and abroad, British nationalized industries were synonymous with over-priced poor-quality service.

However, given that many privatized industries continued to enjoy a significant degree of monopoly power after their transfer into the private sector, it is not immediately clear how precisely privatization was intended to spur incumbent managements to greater efficiency. After all, the morning after privatization, companies like British Telecom and British Gas – with the same managers and staff and effectively unchallenged control of national, integrated distribution networks – faced no greater competition for customers than they had while in the public sector. For such companies, the New Classical economist argued, the impetus to greater competition and efficiency lay in the new vulnerability of privatized enterprises to hostile takeover bids on the stock market.

The problem of natural monopolies

Many of the enterprises that have been privatized are **natural monopolies**, in which the creation of effective competition is highly problematic – see Figure 16.

Moreover, in the case of natural monopolies like electricity, gas and water, not only does the transfer of ownership risk consumer exploitation, but it may also result in the industries becoming less, rather than more, efficient in terms of average production costs. This is because natural monopolies arise in industries that are characterized by declining average cost functions. That is, as output increases, costs continuously decline, so that as soon as one firm grows slightly larger than its rivals, it enjoys a self-reinforcing cost advantage which allows it to grow and cut costs until it has captured the whole market.

Given that, by definition, it is counter-productive to break-up a natural monopoly, the task facing the government is to find a means of transferring such enterprises into the private sector, while at the same time encouraging the new managements to hold down costs and prices. In the UK, as in many other countries, the solution has been to design a system of **regulation** which, to a large extent, replaces the hidden political control of pricing and output decisions that existed in the past.

The role of regulation

The privatized monopolies are regulated by terms laid down in their privatization legislation and their operating licences. For example,

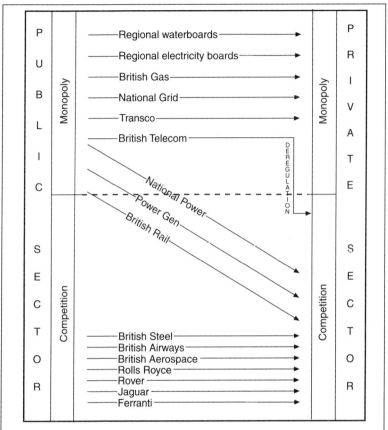

Figure 16 The essential privatizations

Source: B. Hurl, *Privatization and the Public Sector*

British Telecom, which was the first major utility to be privatized, has an operating licence which runs for 25 years in the first instance. This sets out the terms under which the utility must operate, including the supply of rural services, telephone boxes and emergency calls. Prices are largely regulated by a predetermined formula and the regulatory system is policed by the Office of Telecommunications (**OFTEL**). This structure has been copied for gas, water and electricity.

The impact of a regulatory system depends upon its influence on managerial behaviour. In the United States, where private monopoly suppliers of electricity, gas and water have existed for many years, the regulatory system has led to confusion, litigation and, on occasion, commercial disaster. The US regulations variously control the level of service, environmental considerations and pricing, much as in the UK. Three broad problems have been experienced in the United States.

- The system gives too many opportunities to lobbyists and lawyers, who waste resources in lengthy, so-called 'rent-seeking' activities.
- The regulatory agencies in the United States have been criticised for siding with the supplier against the consumer – so-called '**regulatory capture**'.
- Prices have generally been regulated with a view to achieving a 'satisfactory' rate of return on capital, which tends to reduce the incentive for management to control costs, encouraging them to pursue growth and output targets instead of maximizing efficiency.

The method of price control that has been introduced in the UK was designed to overcome the main disadvantages of US-style regulation. The **retail price index (RPI) minus X** formula, as it is known, was intended to control prices while permitting increased profits resulting from lower costs. The regulators would fix the X-factor on the basis of forecast productivity gains in comparable industries (e.g. 2 per cent). If the privatized industry achieved productivity growth in line with this sectoral average, it could then raise its prices each year by 2 per cent *less* than the inflation rate, maintaining a broadly constant rate of return. Productivity improvements in excess of 2 per cent would accordingly enable it to increase its rate of return for the same permitted price rise.

However, despite the advantages of the RPI minus X formula over direct rate-of-return controls, it does contain a major flaw which can lead to precisely the same inefficiencies as US-style regulation. In practice, it appears that the X-factor is periodically reassessed, in the light of what the regulatory body considers to be a 'satisfactory' rate of profit. For example, when BT reported a spectacular rise in its profits in 1991, largely because it had managed to exceed the productivity gains implicit in its X-factor by such an unexpectedly large margin, OFTEL responded to mounting public resentment by threatening to increase the size of the X-factor. Such adjustments, however apparently reasonable on social grounds, may destroy managerial incentives to reduce costs and become more efficient.

The performance of privatized companies

Given that a number of the newly privatized industries have only recently changed their ownership, assessing their performance may prove to be difficult. However, for some of the earlier ones such as British Telecom there may be more concrete evidence on which we can draw. It is important, however, to distinguish between short-run effects and long-run effects, with the latter dealing with **dynamic efficiency gains,** the development of new products and the discovery of new methods of working.

If we consider what has been happening generally to the privatized industries in terms of profits, prices, output and productivity, initial research during the 1980s suggested that performance had generally improved in all these areas, but that the performance gains tended to precede actual privatization. This might beg the question why privatization was needed at all, but it could indicate that the improved performance would not have taken place if privatization was not on the horizon.

Later studies in 1991 considered performance of a number of sectors of the economy in which either ownership *or* control had changed. Performance was measured in terms of labour and total factor productivity, employment and using a range of accounting ratios. Five of the ten cases showed improved performance. However, out of these five, only British Aerospace and the National Freight Corporation had been privatized; the others had improved whilst still in public ownership.

In the case of British Telecom, although productivity rose by an average of 7.5 per cent between 1983 and 1992, some state-owned suppliers in Europe had done almost as well. The evidence for the electricity industry over the same period suggested that privatization had not had a significant impact on productivity growth. The suggestion is, therefore, that improvements in productivity were available to all firms irrespective of type of ownership during the 1980s. Furthermore, how much of any improvement in performance can be related to the buoyant economic conditions of the 1980s or to the level of competition, or lack of it, faced by newly privatized companies?

We have had to wait until the 1990s to begin examining the performance of the newly privatized industries over a time period that not only includes a boom period but also recession. If we examine productivity as a performance indicator once again, and consider British Airways: in the pre-privatization period of 1981–85 and the post-announcement period 1985–87, productivity exceeded that of the late 1970s. However, once past that date productivity has fallen back, registering only 4.8 per cent in the period 1988–92.

British Airports Authority showed a similar trend, and its record of 2.1 per cent between 1988 and 1992 is somewhat disappointing and there have been recent calls for its monopoly to be broken up. For British Telecom the productivity record has been 'onward and upward' since privatization, but here it may be technology rather than ownership that is crucial in controlling performance.

Suppose other performance criteria are examined. Employment has fallen substantially at British Gas, British Steel and British Telecom, but has risen at the British Airports Authority. Some other industries such as British Aerospace have seen their employment levels fluctuate quite widely, being more related to their process of acquisitions and subsequent sales of companies.

There appears to be no confirmed pattern about profitability (not profits), which has risen in some industries and fallen in others after privatization. Though if profits are examined, then some of the industries appear to be very successful. British Telecom made over £3 billion in 1995, the electricity generators in excess of £2 billion, and the electricity distributors and water industries between £1.5 and £2 billion.

These profits may well be reduced in future – not because of the efficiency of the regulators, but as a response to a possible 'windfall' tax by a new government. Utilities are therefore using up spare cash to purchase other firms; hence the bids placed by Scottish Power and Southern Electric for Southern Water in May 1996. Similarly, National Power and Power Gen announced that they would hand back £1.1 billion and £400 million to their shareholders.

Assessing the performance of newly privatized industries is, therefore, not as easy as it at first appears. Prices may be down in real terms, customer care may be further up the agenda, but so are profits. But in terms of other economic measures, it is impossible to say which parts of any productivity gains, employment changes and the like are the result of privatization – rather than a consequence of changes in competition, or improvement in technology. Moreover, pre-privatization productivity gains appear to be better for some organizations than are post-privatization ones, and other comparable state-run enterprises appear to have done almost equally as well.

Conclusions

Privatization has been a central plank of supply side policy during the 1980s and 90s, although the results have been mixed. The attempt to pursue three broad goals – increasing efficiency, widening share ownership and reducing the PSBR – led to inevitable conflicts in policy.

The theoretical case for privatization relies upon a particularly pessimistic view of motivation in the public sector, alongside an optimistic view of the disciplining effect on management of exposure to the commercial capital market.

Economic theory and the international evidence suggest that competition, rather than ownership, is the key to ensuring high operating efficiency. The existence of privatized natural monopolies, which face no significant competition, has necessitated a regulatory structure for each industry. In effect, privatization has simply altered the form of regulation – from political direction to arm's length control by the means of regulatory bodies.

Given the pivotal role of these natural monopolies in the economy, it is difficult to see how any government could abdicate responsibility for their behaviour. Moreover, even if privatization has removed the inefficiencies resulting from direct political intervention, it has introduced new distortions, notably in terms of price control, and opened up the risk of regulatory capture and regulatory muddle.

Assessing the performance of these newly privatized industries is also hazardous. Empirical studies appear to suggest that privatization can improve the performance of nationalized industries, but such improvements are not guaranteed and are more likely to be intertwined with other factors such as changes in competition and demand.

KEY WORDS

Nationalized industries	OFTEL
X-inefficiency	Regulatory capture
Natural monopoly	RPI minus X
Regulation	Dynamic efficiency gains

Reading list

Beharrell, A., 'Privatization: success or failure?', *Economics Today*, September 1994, 4–10.

Burns, J., 'Privatization: what next?', *Economics Today*, September 1991, 4–10.

Hurl, B., *Privatization and the Public Sector*, 3rd edn, Heinemann Educational, 1995.

Smith, D., Chapter 9 in *UK Current Economic Policy*, Heinemann Educational, 1994.

Essay topics

1. (a) What were the expected economic benefits of privatization policy in the UK? [40 marks]
   (b) Using examples, examine the extent to which these benefits have been realized. [60 marks]
   [University of London Examinations and Assessment Council 1995]

2. (a) Explain the benefits which supporters of the government's privatization programme expect to result from the privatization of industries such as gas, water and telecommunications.
   [12 marks]
   (b) To what extent, if any, has the creation of regulatory agencies such as OFGAS, OFWAT and OFTEL minimized the disadvantages of privatization? [13 marks]
   [Associated Examining Board 1995]
3. Explain how in theory price competition affects the economic efficiency of organizations. What basis is there for the view that government policies on internal markets and privatization are likely to be effective in promoting greater economic efficiency in areas such as education, health and rail transport?
   [25 marks]
   [Northern Examinations and Assessment Board 1994]
4. 'The prospects for consumers of gas and electricity have never been better.' Discuss. [25 marks]
   [Oxford & Cambridge Schools Examination Board 1996]

Data Response Question

This task is based on a question set by the University of London Examinations and Assessment Council in 1996. Read the article, which is adapted from 'The role of the regulators' in *The Economist* of 1 June 1991. Then answer the questions.

1. Discuss the factors that a regulator might take into account when deciding whether or not the profits made by a utility such as BT or a water company are too high. [7 marks]
2. Using the example of *either* gas *or* telecommunications, explain and illustrate the term 'vertical integration'. [4 marks]
3. Discuss the advantages and disadvantages of breaking up the electricity industry into separate companies for generating and distributing electricity. [6 marks]
4. Examine the possible effects on the efficiency of a privatized utility of *one* of the following regulatory policy measures referred to in the passage:
   (a) the 'RPI minus X' pricing rule;
   (b) 'yardstick' competition; *or*
   (c) 'unbundling' costs and prices. [8 marks]

The regulation of privatized industries

Big profits mean bad regulation. Or so you would think from the outcry that greeted British Telecom's announcement that its profits in 1990–91 were £31.1 billion, which is equivalent to £97 per second. Much of the current uproar is due to a simple confusion between big – which the monopoly's profits certainly are – and too big. BT is Britain's biggest, most valuable and most profitable firm. But its profits are a relatively small proportion of sales (at 21.5 per cent) and of capital (21.3 per cent).

Even so, some of the privatised monopolies' profits may well be too high. The regulators certainly think so. Their main method of control is the pricing formula known as 'RPI minus X'. This means that each firm must limit its product price rises to X percentage points less than the rate of inflation. If the regulator reckons that a firm is earning too much monopoly profit, it can raise X. So far, the regulators have raised X each time they have reviewed it.

This is no surprise. To get public sector managers to agree to be privatized, and to persuade investors to buy the shares, the government had to offer incentives to the newly-privatized companies. In the case of the water companies, managers were encouraged to believe that they would be able to raise their prices to cover the costs of almost any investment. Once privatized, the government has little reason to preserve such a friendly policy and every reason to make life tougher since consumers are voters.

'RPI minus X' can work if the regulator has a good idea of how efficient the firm is, and how much better it could be. This is most likely when technology is fairly mature, so that the rate at which the regulators learn about the firm is faster than the rate at which the firm changes. In most of the UK's regulated monopolies, technology changes slowly as with gas pipes, water pipes, runways and so on. The big exception is telecommunications, where technology is changing fast.

Promoting competition should be the aim of the regulators, even in technologically mature industries. The UK still lacks a clear policy on vertical integration. Electricity has been broken into competitive generation and monopoly distributors, but gas and telecommunications remain more integrated. 'Yardstick' competition – comparing the performance of one local monopoly with other similar monopolies – has been considered by the regulators for some time, but it has still to be seriously used. 'Unbundling' the costs and prices of all a firm's activities – as BT began to do when it charged for directory enquiries and cut ordinary call charges – reduces unnecessary regulation and should go much further.

Chapter Eight

Competition and improving markets

'The 1990s promised to witness a further bonfire of regulatory obstacles to free competition ...'

Introduction

Although the privatization of public utilities by the various Conservative administrations received the greatest headlines, other areas of the public sector had market relationships introduced or were deregulated in the hope that this would increase competition, improve efficiency and, at a macro level, help to increase national output and reduce inflation.

At the same time there were also forces at work in the wider economic community which were helping to reduce the frictions between markets, such as the Single European Market, the eighth round of GATT, and the further development of regional trading blocs which were to have longer-term but still profound effects on the demands placed upon British industry.

Contracting-out

Large nationalized industries were viewed with suspicion. Also, Conservative perceptions were that local authorities were inefficient and so wasted public money, as well as being unaccountable and a threat to political stability. For example, Labour councils could undermine Conservative government budgetary control. In order to reduce this **countervailing power**, local authorities were subject to rate-capping, a change to the poll tax, and the introduction of contracting-out or competitive tendering.

Compulsory Competitive Tendering (CCT) was introduced by the Local Government Planning and Land Act 1980. CCT covered services such as highways, buildings and maintenance work. This process was taken further in 1988 under the Local Government Act, which extended CCT to refuse collection, cleaning, catering, ground maintenance and vehicle maintenance.

Local authorities were required to put contracts out to competitive tendering, where one of the tenders could be made by the present staff. Where multiple tenders were received, at least three had to be considered and the local authority was not able to specify constraints within the contract such as guaranteeing previous wage rates and insisting that the workforce be unionized. The dominant factor in agreeing the contract was that a minimum rate of return on capital of 5 per cent should be expected.

The results of the process of contracting-out have been mixed. Almost three-quarters of contracts put out to tender have been won by in-house bids. There have been variations by service, with around 70 per cent of refuse and street collection contracts, over 95 per cent of catering contracts, and around 55 per cent of building and cleaning contracts, remaining in-house. In a survey carried out in 1991, it was found that the majority of contracting-out occurred in Conservative-controlled Rural District Councils.

Some local authorities used the threat of competition to push through deterioration in employees' terms and conditions of employment. As to the efficiency gains, studies appeared to show conflicting reports. All noted that costs tended to be lower after the contract had been won through the competitive tendering process; but as to whether contracting-out gave the greater cost reduction as compared with the contract remaining in-house, the surveys are not conclusive.

Nonetheless, the surveys did suggest that cost reductions were more likely to arise through reductions in wages and longer hours, rather than through efficiency gains.

Why were many of the contracts won by in-house bids? This was due partly to lack of interest by the private sector, partly to lack of capacity by that sector, partly to a fear of failure because of the high risks involved, and the high cost of entry owing to lack of management expertise or cost of capital. In addition, it should be noted that on a number of occasions complaints arose after the service had been contracted out.

The process of contracting-out has been effectively halted since 1993 because CCT might have been carried out in breach of EU law.

Market relationships in schools and the NHS

The Conservative government has tried to get different departments or components within a particular part of the public sector to trade with one another, as a means of encouraging competition and efficiency. Two of the best examples of this can be found in education and the health service.

One way of doing this was to use devolved budgets. Schools, under the LMS (**local management of schools**) scheme, have to all intents and purposes become self-financing. They have been given their own bud-

gets, out of which they must meet the bills for teachers' salaries and many other costs. It is hoped that this will encourage schools to cut costs and thereby reduce the burden for taxpayers. As a response to this, schools have looked to encourage some of their older and more experienced teachers to take early retirement and have replaced them with younger, cheaper, less experienced members of staff.

Perhaps the most comprehensive introduction of market relationships can be found in the health service. As an attempt to reduce costs, the Thatcher administration saw the NHS as an important sector for its supply side reforms. The 1989 White Paper *Working for Patients* aimed to introduce market disciplines into the NHS, improving efficiency and reducing costs. The White Paper presented the case for the development of an **internal market** within the NHS using the following reforms:

- Provision of healthcare was devolved from regional health authorities to individual hospitals.
- NHS hospitals could seek Trust status, giving them greater control over staff pay, borrowing of funds and the use of profits, and choice over which medical services to provide.
- Hospitals could offer their services to all district health authorities and the private sector.
- GPs could control their budgets, and purchase services for patients directly from hospitals.
- The NHS was to be managed in a more business-like fashion.

GP's budgets are related to the size of their practice and their 'needs', given its location and the demographic structure of its patients. GPs have an incentive to be efficient since any money left at the end of the year can be used in their practice. Hospitals can attract business by adjusting the prices of their treatments, as well as using non-price factors such as the lengths of their waiting lists.

In judging the success of the reforms, advocates suggest that these will only be seen in the long term. On the other hand, some GP practices have grown, leading to economies of scale; and as larger purchasers of treatment the GPs are able to yield greater **monopsony power**. In addition GPs can use their position to seek hospitals on the basis of performance indicators such as death rates, waiting lists and hospital star ratings based upon time factors such as length of time in outpatients etc.

Deregulation

Some privatizations have been accompanied by **deregulation,** and it is often argued that it is the latter, rather than the former, that actually promotes competition.

Deregulation involves reducing the number of regulations by removing those that serve only to restrict competition and do little to enhance the safety of customers or workers. The objectives of deregulation are to increase competition between existing suppliers and between them and new suppliers who can now enter the market. This should reduce costs and stimulate the provision of new services for which there is a demand. Recent examples of deregulation in the UK are buses and in the EU the 'single market'.

The Transport Act 1980 deregulated long-distance coach travel. Restrictions on operators entering the market were removed and limited to safety standards. Many small companies entered the market, which was until then dominated by the state-owned National Bus Company. The latter fought back successfully by cutting its fares and introducing new routes. There has been a significant fall in long-distance coach fares and a consequent rise in the number of passenger-miles travelled.

In 1986, local bus services were deregulated. Until then private operators had been unable to enter the market without securing a local authority licence for the route. Under the new legislation local authorities are required to tender for their local bus routes and award the tender to the cheapest contractor. Subsidies to bus services have also been cut. The objective of the legislation is to reduce the costs of bus travel and to provide those services for which there is a local demand by allowing the entry of small operators.

Deregulation and '1992': the EU single market

The 1990s promised to witness a further bonfire of regulatory obstacles to free competition on an altogether wider scale. The European Union's so-called '1992' programme to complete the '**single market**' was scheduled for completion by 31 December 1992.

In its attempt to create a genuinely free market in goods, services, labour and capital, the European Union aims to either harmonize or abolish a wide range of official restrictions and regulations that tend to act as 'non-tariff barriers' – protecting small, inefficient national pro-

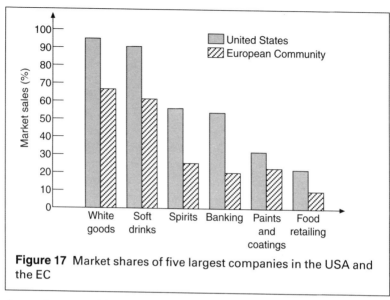

Figure 17 Market shares of five largest companies in the USA and the EC

ducers from outside competition.

The fundamental problem is that centuries of separate political development by the 15 member states have spawned mutually inconsistent sets of legislation on technical and health and safety standards. This segments the EU into small, discrete markets served by small-scale producers.

For example, the EU has 50 tractor manufacturers competing for annual sales of 200 000 units. In the United States, a *market of similar size* is served by only four large producers! In the EU, it was almost impossible to manufacture a tractor that would sell in more than two or three countries without significant engineering alterations.

Figure 17 shows that this pattern is replicated across other industrial sectors such as white goods, soft drinks, and alcoholic beverages.

Inconsistent national standards therefore fragment the market and perpetuate inefficient small-scale production.

The prices of 'tradeable' goods and services still vary widely across EU countries. *In an integrated market, differences should reflect only transport costs when expressed in a common currency, reflecting the 'law of one price'.* Once the 1992 measures have been fully implemented, competition within the EU is likely to intensify dramatically, driving prices down and strengthening the supply side of the EU as a whole.

Assessing the outcome of the 'single market'

The lists of *potential* costs and benefits that arise from enacting the various pieces of the Single European Act (SEA) are extensive. The *benefits* include:

- economies of scale;
- increased competition both in the short run and long run;
- gains from reduction in X-inefficiency (see Chapter 7);
- trade creation.

The *costs* include:

- adverse regional multiplier effects;
- the problems of radical economic change that can occur through efficiency and scale gains.

What the OECD thinks

If the first achievement of the Tory governments since 1979 was to stop the UK's relative economic decline, many economists identify a second that may prove of even greater significance. They claim that various reforms introduced during this period have raised the average rate at which GDP can grow over the long-run without pushing up inflation. The government has increased the trend growth rate it uses in its forecasts, and the OECD has done likewise. If this is correct, the UK may soon soar up the world prosperity league.

The OECD, among others, argues that greater labour-market flexibility resulting from Tory attacks on union privileges, reforms of labour law and tighter rules on unemployment benefits have helped to create extremely favourable conditions for creating jobs quickly (hence the early fall in unemployment in this recovery) and without pushing up inflation.

The OECD also argues that the UK has benefited in recent years from being more exposed to competitive forces than many rival economies. This is due to the creation of Europe's single market, to privatization and deregulation, and to changes in industrial structure following the prompt adoption of new technologies.

That is largely true. However, unless the UK pursues a more vigorous anti-trust policy at home, many of these gains could evaporate.

Adapted from *The Economist*, 8 June 1996

Free trade and trading blocs

The changes that arose through the 'single market' encouraged trade between the EU member states. However, on a wider international stage, 'supply-siders' saw that great benefits could be achieved by continuing to remove barriers to wider world trade.

The eighth GATT round – the **Uruguay Round** – attempted to target a whole range of issues that would help in liberalizing markets. The results of the trade talks are estimated to bring an estimated increase in world income of US$510 billion per year by the time the market access commitments are fully implemented.

- There is expected to be an increase in income following the tariff reductions and other liberalizing actions, which should stimulate world trade, investment and production. The estimated annual income gains are $122 billion for the US, $164 billion for the EU, $27 billion for Japan and $116 billion for developing and transition economies.
- It is projected that there will be a 40 per cent reduction in tariffs imposed by developed countries on incoming industrial goods, with the proportion of industrial products entering these markets under Most Favoured Nation zero duties more than doubling from 20 to 44 per cent.
- Removal of quantitative restrictions on products are expected, particularly textiles and clothing.
- There is expected to be a reduction in import barriers on agricultural products – in particular a reduction in export subsidies and improved market access.
- Market access should be made more secure through 'bindings'. That is, once a tariff is reduced on a product then the country agrees to bind the tariff, committing itself not to increase the tariff above that level.
- There is to be a commitment to lower barriers on services. The General Agreement on Trade in Services (GATS) is the first multilateral agreement covering trade in all service sectors. By providing for secure access to markets and progressive liberalization, it will stimulate the growth of services trade in the same way that GATT did for goods.

Thus although the Uruguay Round took eight years to bring to a conclusion, the scope of its agreements went a long way in the direction of freer trade. On the other hand, the world is certainly not yet one of totally free trade.

Competition policy

On both a UK and a pan-European level, there has been a tendency for large firms to develop through market forces – seeking all the scale advantages of being big. This has been paralleled by some governments and the European Commission in trying to develop larger European firms to compete better on the world stage with both Japanese and American multinationals.

Allowing such firms to develop may give them distinct advantages, *but at the same time it provides the opportunity for markets to behave inefficiently.* These inefficiencies have been looked at earlier, in the context of the arguments for privatization, but here we shall recall three points:

- Large firms may use resources inefficiently.
- Because they dominate markets they may abuse this power by charging higher prices and producing lower levels of output than firms would under competitive conditions in the same market.
- Large firms may under-invest in both labour training and investment.

Thus there are supply side problems. But what type of competition policy might be developed? There are no hard and fast rules, but there may be some useful starting points.

Differences in **market structure** may affect the competitive behaviour of firms. Markets that are highly competitive are unlikely to lead to organizations whose performance could reduce market welfare. On the other hand, it is not always possible to say that markets that are oligopolistic, or where there is a single provider, will lead to reductions in economic welfare. Oligopolists, for example, can behave both competitively and cooperatively.

Consideration should also be given to **contestability** of markets. Evidence which shows the movement of firms into and out of an industry may suggest that the market is contestable and that economic welfare is not being harmed. Conversely, where markets do not appear to be contestable then entry barriers may be being used and competition policy needs to consider how these barriers can be reduced.

Competition policy, therefore, should be designed to promote more competition or to prevent a reduction in competition. Economists differ as to the market conditions necessary to best promote competition – that is either through market forces or through the direct involvement of the government – and it follows that the types of competition policy advocated differ.

If we are concerned about market structure and the ramifications that flow from this, then competition policy should attempt to change market structure and impose constraints on the behaviour of firms. That is:

- barriers to entry should be reduced;
- monopolies should be broken-up or regulated;
- there should be attempts to stop organizations reaching a dominant position through a mergers policy.

Competition policy should thus actively prevent organizations from abusing their dominant market positions via restrictive practices.

Assessing UK competition policy

It is sometimes difficult to separate the effects of competition policy from other changes that are taking place, such as **globalization** (the internationalization of markets), changes in technology, likely changes in aggregate demand and the like.

It should also be noted that, in the case of *mergers*, fewer than 50 per cent have met the criteria for investigation. Of these, under 3 per cent have been referred to the Monopolies & Mergers Commission (MMC); and of these around 60 per cent have either been refused permission or have been abandoned. Overall, just about 1 per cent of mergers have been deemed not to be in the public interest.

There have even been cases where the recommendations of the Director General of Fair Trading have been overruled. In 1991, for example, the BPB group, Europe's largest plasterboard manufacturer, was prevented by the Director General from taking over the French building materials group Poilet. However, the government felt that competition would not be harmed and overruled the decision.

With regard to the UK's policy on mergers, the principle of having to prove that a merger is against the public interest has been questioned. *Some have argued that the boot should be on the other foot – that it should be proved that a merger is for the public interest before it is allowed.*

Since 1980 there has been a shift in emphasis in merger policy. Apart from the statutory 'market share' criterion, recommendations to the MMC have reflected the implications from the changes in competition that could follow from the merger being granted. Such an approach was adopted in the attempted takeover of the Midland Bank by Lloyds.

During the 1990s, UK merger policy appears to be moving closer to that established throughout the EU, with a greater consideration of establishing **national champions** as a way of competing in global markets. *Here, industrial policy may now be in conflict with competition policy.*

Conclusions

- Addressing inefficiency in the local authority sector has had mixed results. Many contracts are still in-house, though they cost less. However, whether this is due to the lower cost base, or to existing resources being used more efficiently, is a moot point.

- Introduction of market forces into the NHS has come at the same time that demographic demands are increasing on the service. It would appear that efficiency has improved, but some have argued that there is little fat left to trim.
- On a wider level, UK competition policy has been used to improve the competitiveness of organizations, yet there is doubt expressed as to its consistency in decision-making, and further whether the process has become more biased towards establishing national champions.
- On the international front, the working through of the 'single market', the satisfactory conclusion of the Uruguay trade talks, and the development of trading blocs, have triggered and sustained important supply side changes in a global context.

One lesson to be noted here is that international changes to help the supply side may not always parallel domestic changes, and the former may result in the latter being undertaken.

KEY WORDS

Countervailing power	Single market
Compulsory Competitive Tendering	Uruguay Round
	Competition policy
Local management of schools	Market structure
Internal market	Contestability
Monopsony power	Globalization
Performance indicators	National champions
Deregulation	

Reading list

Hurl, B., Chapters 3 and 6 in *Privatization and the Public Sector*, 3rd edn, Heinemann Educational, 1995.

Mason, T., 'Competition policy: does it exist?', *Economics Today*, 1995, 22–26.

Essay topics

1. (a) Explain briefly the meaning of the terms 'barriers to entry' and 'barriers to exit'. [30 marks]

   (b) How might barriers to entry be expected to affect the way in which markets operate in the real world? Illustrate your answer with relevant examples. [70 marks]

   [University of London Examinations and Assessment Council 1996]

2. (a) In a market economy, prices (i) give signals to participants in the economy; (ii) act as a rationing device; (iii) provide incentives. Explain *each* of these functions. [12 marks]

   (b) Evaluate the economic arguments *for* and *against* introducing a system where schools charge their own fees and the government gives parents a voucher for each child which is used to contribute towards the school fees. [13 marks]

   [Associated Examining Board 1995]

3. Economies of scale result in large companies that dominate the market. Competition is thus reduced and, therefore, exploitation of the consumer is inevitable.

   (a) Examine the economic issues raised in this argument. [15 marks]

   (b) Discuss the extent to which you agree with it. [10 marks]

   [University of Cambridge Local Examinations Syndicate 1996]

4. How in theory should the single European market improve the economy of Europe? Discuss whether or not the benefits from these improvements are likely to be shared equally by the participating nations. [25 marks]

   [Northern Examinations and Assessment Board 1995]

5. Have the reforms of the National Health Service increased patient choice and improved the availability of services? [25 marks]

   [Oxford & Cambridge Schools Examination Board 1996]

Data Response Question

This task is based on a question set by the University of London Examinations and Assessment Council in 1996. Study Tables A and B and then answer the questions that follow.

Table A. National newspaper circulation in the UK

Title of newspaper	Owned by	Daily circulation 1992	1993	1994
Sun	News Corporation	3 588 077	3 513 591	4 007 520
Daily Mirror	Headington Investment	2 868 263	2 676 015	2 484 436
Daily Mail	Daily Mail	1 688 808	1 769 253	1 784 030
Daily Express	United Newspapers	1 537 726	1 490 323	1 369 266
Daily Telegraph	Ravelston Corporation	1 043 703	1 024 340	1 007 944
Daily Star	United Newspapers	808 486	773 908	746 412
Today	News Corporation	495 405	533 332	579 910
Guardian	Guardian Newspapers	418 026	416 207	400 399
Times	News Corporation	390 323	368 219	471 847
Independent	Newspaper Publishing	376 532	348 692	284 440
Financial Times	Pearson	291 915	290 139	296 984
Totals		13 507 264	13 204 019	13 433 188

Table B UK newspaper price reductions in early 1993

	Old price	New price
Sun	25p	20p
Times	45p	20p
Daily Telegraph	48p	30p

1. With reference to Table A, comment on the view that News Corporation was a monopoly in the market for national daily newspapers in 1994. [3 marks]
2. Suggest *two* reasons why some newspaper companies publish more than one newspaper title. [4 marks]
3. Some of the other newspaper publishers considered that the price reductions announced by News Corporation for *The Sun* and *The Times* were an example of predatory pricing.
   (a) Explain what is meant by 'predatory pricing'. [3 marks]
   (b) Examine *three* reasons which might explain why News Corporation embarked on such a pricing policy.
4. To what extent might newspaper publishing be regarded as a contestable market? [5 marks]
5. In the UK, newspaper publishers are prevented from controlling domestic independent television companies. Why might newspaper publishers seek to expand into other media? [4 marks]

Conclusion

'Supply side economics [is] *common sense ... Economists have long recognised the importance of an economy's productive capacity – its stock of labour and capital and the incentives needed to get the best out of them ... Marx was in many respects a supply side economist.'*
The Economist

There is nothing new about 'supply side economics'. Although the term came into common usage only relatively recently, the idea that governments should direct economic policies towards strengthening the supply side dates back to Adam Smith. Indeed, according to Colin Harbury and Richard Lipsey:

> *'supply side economics ... is what Adam Smith's* Wealth of Nations *was all about.'*

The argument has always been over the best means to achieve the end of a vital supply side, rather than over the end itself.

Until the 1930s, governments believed that the best way to promote economic growth was to provide a stable, *laissez-faire* business environment in which private sector activity could flourish. During the depression of the interwar years, faith in the ability of free markets to deliver economic prosperity was badly dented. The so-called 'Keynesian revolution' overturned the apparently discredited classical orthodoxy, encouraging postwar governments to intervene directly in the supply side to achieve their objectives for growth.

In recent years, however, the pendulum has swung back, with the New Classical 'counter-revolution' challenging the Keynesian approach to the supply side. Under the guidance of New Classical economists, governments around the world have set about dismantling the apparatus of state regulation and control, in an attempt to breath life back into the market forces they charge excessive government with having suffocated.

In the UK, the results of this intellectual backlash against state intervention in the supply side have been mixed. Output and productivity growth both improved in the 1980s relative to the period 1973–79, but failed to regain the momentum enjoyed during the 1960s – when the Keynesian era was at its zenith. Industrial relations have undoubtedly benefited from the new legislative framework introduced by the Conservative government and strikes have fallen to record lows. On the other hand, investment in both physical and human capital – training and education – remains well below the levels taken for granted in other advanced economies, and R&D is on a downward trend.

The Holy Grail of higher growth

Britain's economy grew by a thumping 3.9 per cent in 1994, but neither the government nor the opposition (nor, indeed, the voters) reckon such rapid growth can last. Most estimates suggest that, over the long run, the economy can grow only at a more leisurely $2\frac{1}{4}$ per cent a year without whipping up an inflationary storm. So, on 22 May both of Britain's main parties unveiled new packages of policies promising to help the economy do better. Tony Blair, the Labour leader, spelt out in more detail how he would create a 'high success economy'. And Michael Heseltine, the president of the Board of Trade, launched a glossy white paper on boosting competitiveness, claiming that 'we need to raise our game'.

So both parties now promise to eschew the sort of fiscal and monetary policies that have so often led to boom and bust in the past, and to concentrate instead on the kind of microeconomic changes which might, in the long term, actually raise the ability of the British economy to grow. That is splendid. But delivering on those promises will not be easy. Short-term political considerations will always tempt a government to relax macroeconomic discipline. Worse, the microeconomic changes that might actually enable the economy to grow faster in the long term are often contentious and require a great deal of patience. It takes a far-sighted, and determined, politician to push through changes which may look small, and for

which he may never receive much credit. British voters should be encouraged by the shift of attention in both parties to supply-side measures, but should also remain sceptical.

Therefore even on supply-side measures the devil is in the detail. Fortunately neither party is any longer espousing the aggressive industrial policies of the past. Nevertheless, Labour believes that the economy is in a much worse condition than does the government, and thus it proposes more activism. The government points out, rightly, that productivity has risen more rapidly in Britain than in most OECD countries during the past 15 years and that Britain has maintained its share of world exports, in an expanding market, since the early 1980s. This, it says, owes much to its curbing of trade-union power and its investment in education and training.

Labour, by contrast, largely dismisses the government's supply-side reforms of the 1980s. It thinks recent productivity gains may be no more than the 'battling average' effect – increasing productivity per head by shedding less-productive workers – and may not last as unemployment falls. Export growth may reflect the weakness of sterling. It believes big reforms are still needed to improve the labour market, encourage firms to invest more (total investment in Britain remains low by OECD standards), and increase competition.

Abridged from *The Economist*, 27 May 1995

Against this background, the indications are that a process of convergence towards a more balanced approach to supply side policy is likely to prevail over the rest of this century. While New Classical, free market policies have strengthened the supply side in certain areas, such as labour relations, the experience of the 1980s has revealed important limitations in the *laissez-faire* philosophy.

As we saw in Chapter 3, some types of economic activity are plagued by market failure: private companies are loath to train workers, since it is more cost-effective, at the level of the individual company, to free-ride in the hope that rivals will train staff that can subsequently be poached. Similarly, it is cheaper to wait for other firms to pay for pioneering R&D, producing cheaper imitation products once the new technology has been perfected.

There is no doubt that supply side policies have caused major changes in the UK economy, and perhaps the rise in the UK's percentage of world exports is evidence that they are working, though this may be due more to the growth in foreign production in the UK. This improvement, albeit small, shows the UK has a long way to go before it can once again match its major rivals.

The Holy Grail is higher growth – see the article from *The Economist*. The supply side reforms of the past few years have enabled John Bull, although puffing and panting, to stay in the race. *Can he catch up?*

Index